Ozark Hideaways

Ozark Hideaways

Twenty-Seven Day Trips
for Hiking and Fishing

Louis C. White

University of Missouri Press
Columbia and London

Copyright © 1993 by
The Curators of the University of Missouri
University of Missouri Press, Columbia, Missouri 65201
Printed and bound in the United States of America
All rights reserved
5   4   3   2   1   97   96   95   94   93

Library of Congress Cataloging-in-Publication Data

White, Louis C., 1934–
    Ozark hideaways : twenty-seven day trips for hiking and fishing /
Louis C. White.
        p.   cm.
    Includes index.
    ISBN 0-8262-0903-3 (pbk.)
    1. Hiking—Ozark Mountain Region—Guidebooks. 2. Fishing—
Ozark Mountain Region—Guidebooks. 3. Ozark Mountain
Region—Guidebooks. I. Title.
GV199.42.O96W47   1993
796.5'09767'1—dc20
                                                                93-28732
                                                                CIP

♾™ This paper meets the minimum requirements of
the American National Standard for Permanence of Paper
for Printed Library Materials, Z39.48, 1984.

Designer: Rhonda Miller
Typesetter: Connell-Zeko Type & Graphics
Printer and binder: Walsworth Publishing Company
Typefaces: Melliza and Linda

Searching

Fog slips down the hill
And gathers in fragile pools
That soften reality.
Light awakens the meadow.
Shadows flee the dawn.
A wealth of dew shimmers on leaf
And trembling blade.
Bird songs call the morning
To fill an empty day.
The river whispers
Secrets I hope to understand
Again.
I give myself to the dawn
And follow the ghosts
Of stolen dreams
That I would live anew;
That I would find
In solitude.

CONTENTS

PREFACE

If you have grown tired of seeing as many people as trees when you go hiking; if the waters you visit seem to have more lures in them than fish; if your nature photographs at times recall the bustle of a New York subway; if you yearn for a haven off the beaten path—take heart. There are streams and trails where the loudest sounds are the snort of a deer surprised at your intrusion, the splash of feeding fish, and the bleating of a beaver family under an overhanging bank. There are small valleys that still echo the cries of a soaring hawk, where the most obtrusive sign of civilization is a dairy herd grazing on the lush grass of a tree-lined meadow.

If you become melancholy when you haven't heard a car horn for a few hours; if you don't like to tote a pack for miles just to earn the privilege of sleeping on a gravel bar with frogs and owls as company; if you don't pick up after yourself or careless people who have gone before you—close this book and go to a crowded campground. You wouldn't be interested in the places I describe.

If you want to catch a mess of trophy-sized fish, these spots are also not for you: game fish populations are not usually overwhelming. Fishing as you wade and explore can enliven an outing but should not be the foremost reason for the trip. Although I do occasionally catch impressive fish in small waters or find them feeding so actively that I could fill stringer after stringer, I return nearly every fish I take so it remains for another day. There are plenty of other places that can readily provide for a fish fry.

But if you have some vestige of pioneering spirit and cherish quiet times with nature, alone or with one or two understanding friends; if you care for the environment and do your best to leave it better than you found it—

then read on. The streams I describe here are what you have been seeking.

For over twenty years I have fished and hiked the streams of southern Missouri and northern Arkansas. To escape increasing tourist pressure, I have fled from the crowds farther and farther upstream, back into the hills. Away from the heavily frequented spots, I have discovered sanctuaries in the headwaters and tributaries of Ozark streams.

Most people ignore the possibilities of these secluded upstream areas, where the scenery is quite often more spectacular than the view along the broader waters below. There are icy springs and isolated mills, noisy waterfalls and churning rapids, cliffs dotted with caves, and intimate canyons offering deep, mossy pools along the tiniest of streams. These wondrous places await those who are willing to go farther and work harder to reach them.

I wish to thank: Lisa Fann, an English teacher at Liberty High School, Mountain View, Missouri, for her invaluable help in the writing of this book; my map artist, Mendy McNew; my family, all my friends, and the members of my high school classes for their patience and support during my initiation into the unknown perils of writing a book.

Ozark Hideaways

REGIONAL MAP

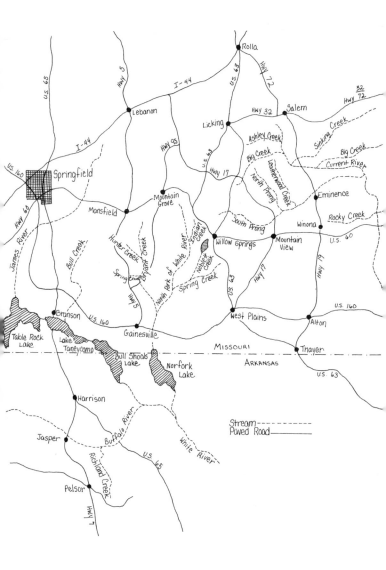

INTRODUCTION ═══════════════════

     This book describes some of my favorite hikes down little-known streams in the Missouri and Arkansas Ozarks, and attempts to convey some sense of their distinctive beauty. I hope that those who already have a fondness for such places will be prompted to pay some of these a visit. Even more, I would like to introduce a distinctive approach to nature for readers who have never hiked or waded small streams. The scenery along these streams varies from the cozy and intimate to the amazingly spectacular. For those who appreciate unique pleasures far from the crowd, some part of every one of these hikes will provide another fond memory.

I call attention to the obvious and some of the not-so-obvious points of interest along these streams. Quite a few of them have unusual attractions that many local residents don't even know about. Scattered throughout the book are odds and ends of local history as well as personal memories associated with certain hikes, and most chapters include descriptions of interesting plants and animals. My account has been drawn from extensive experience over the years, and I have made at least one additional visit to each stream before writing about it so that the information is as recent as possible.

To help those unfamiliar with this part of the Ozarks to find their way, I have included detailed maps of the hikes along every stream I describe, indicating the relevant highways and back roads leading to them. I refer frequently to easily identified landmarks and often give distances and travel times along the way. This should make it simple to judge how far you have left to go at any point on your trip and enable you to pace yourself and budget your time accordingly.

The hikes are designed to take from a half to the better part of a day, but many factors can influence that time. Much depends upon your age and physical condition. Walking through gravel, sand, and water makes it hard to average over a mile and a half an hour. Fishing and photography can slow you down even further. If you have a vehicle waiting at the other end, where that is possible, a one-way hike can cut the time in half or give you more time for sight-seeing and fishing.

Round-trips of ten to sixteen miles make for a full day of hiking; they also take a good deal of endurance and account for many a sore muscle. Remember that wading is harder than normal walking and exercises different muscles. Even hikers in the best shape can develop cramps in the groin, hamstring, or arches. Blisters and stone bruises on the feet are always a hazard and can quickly hobble anyone. If you don't walk a great deal, you should build up your endurance before attempting any of the trips described in this book. Of course, any hike can be lengthened or shortened to suit individual needs.

I usually follow one of two patterns during my own hikes. If I am fishing, I walk up or down the stream as far as I judge reasonable for the time I have available, then fish my way back to my truck. I allow about twice the time for the return trip of fishing and sight-seeing as I took for the steady hike on my way out. If I am on a nature hike and doing a little photography, I explore the hills and valleys on one side of the stream on my way out and walk the other side on my return.

There are a few precautions to keep in mind and some minor preparation before you embark on any of these walks. For instance, you should always inform someone of the plans for your hike. In the unlikely event that an accident occurs, it is good to know someone will come looking when you are overdue.

Care should be taken at any time of the year along all

Ozark streams when thunderstorms threaten. Park your vehicle well above signs of high water, which can rise to astonishing levels with frightening speed even on small watersheds. Be ready to leave the water and climb a handy bank at the first sign of turbulence and discoloration in the stream, even if it is not raining where you are. A low, rumbling noise from upstream should be cause for immediate concern and action. During a flash flood a few years ago, I saw a car washed completely into Lake Taneycomo from a gravel bar along Bull Creek.

Always take a raincoat with you, even in the summer. It is surprising how cold you can get when you are caught out in a strong thunderstorm. Even if the air temperature is not low, hypothermia is an ever-present danger when you are wet. Besides, dry clothes are infinitely more comfortable than soggy attire.

Carry plenty of water. If you wear waders, you will perspire inside them, even in the winter. In hot weather the threat of dehydration is more obvious. Stop often for a drink and carry snacks that are high in water content, such as citrus fruits and apples. Never drink water from streams or springs without first purifying it by one of the standard methods: boiling, filtering with an appropriate system, or adding iodine tablets.

There are many caves along the watersheds of the streams I describe, and a few words of caution are in order if you decide to venture into any of them. It is not prudent to explore a cave when you are alone. The wisest course is to find an experienced spelunker to accompany you on any expeditions that proceed much beyond the entrance of a cavern. Proper equipment, such as a hard hat to cushion against bumps of the head and footwear that ensures secure footing, is a must. Cave floors are often slippery and uneven, and the danger of falls is great. Take more than one flashlight with you; one that can be worn on the head is very useful, freeing your hands to help maintain your balance. Don't go very far down branching passages unless you have some dependable means of marking your path, such as unreeling a long spool of strong line behind you. Never mark on cave walls or floors, and avoid contact with the delicate cave formations: they grow at an extremely slow rate and even the slightest amount of body oil from your fingers can stop their growth completely.

Be extremely careful around elevated ledges and other drop-offs—the slightest misstep can have dire consequences. Rock-climbing on the many precipitous bluffs and canyons along Ozark streams is a temptation to the hiker, but it presents a great danger to the inexperienced. Without the proper skills and equipment, the likelihood of falls is more than a minor worry. Those who become injured on solitary hikes in isolated areas may find it difficult or impossible to find help or get back to their vehicle.

Snakes, even the less common poisonous ones, are not a serious problem if you use ordinary caution. On a few rare occasions I have encountered a blacksnake that was a little belligerent and turned to face me threateningly after it had fled a few feet. Some friends have told me that cottonmouths can act this way too, but any snake will give way if you threaten it with your staff. If you must walk through overgrown areas that make it hard to see where you are stepping, go slowly and move your hiking staff back and forth along the ground in front of you. Anything hidden in the weeds will probably disappear long before you arrive.

I strongly recommend that you carry and use a hiking or wading staff. If you have never used one, you can't imagine the help they are—both in and out of the water. While you are hiking, they transfer some of the effort from legs to arms, making you much more stable and less likely to slip and stumble on uneven or rocky ground. Staffs are as much use in slowing your descent down steep slopes as they are in helping you climb them. In the water, a staff lessens your chance of slipping on slick rocks, and it is indispensable when you wade across a swiftly flowing stream.

Most recently I have used a staff made from a straight oak sapling cut from the woods on my farm. Some seven feet long, it has a smoothed shaft, a top formed into a rounded knob, and a handy grip carved farther down for two-handed use. Some people prefer a shorter staff and some prefer a cane. I think a longer staff is safer because it prevents injuries caused by falling against the end of your own staff when you slip. Try different types for yourself and see which you prefer.

It is handy to secure the staff to your belt with a heavy nylon cord so that it can be released when you are using both hands for fishing but is still easy to retrieve when needed. Tie the cord above the middle of your staff so that it will return to your hand in the correct position when you pull it up. The cord should be long enough to enable you to use it comfortably with either hand, but short enough to avoid tangling your legs when you walk. As unlikely as it may seem, the cord very seldom tangles in the brush.

Wading outfits should be kept simple—the lighter, the better. I wear lightweight neoprene waders (so-called stocking-foot waders) in cold weather, with high-top canvas basketball shoes over their feet. Underwear made of a "wicking" fabric worn under the waders helps carry perspiration away from your legs and keeps the inside of the waders dryer. Wading boots prove awkward when you are walking long distances, they tend to be expensive, and they wear out much faster than ordinary tennis shoes. As the weather warms up, I prefer to wade in jeans and the same high-top canvas shoes. This outfit is much lighter than waders, and side trips away from the stream are much easier. Not having to protect fragile waders from thorns and limbs that snag and tear is another significant advantage. Setting aside a change of clothing, including dry socks and shoes, at the end of your hike will leave you much more comfortable on your way home.

Everything carried in your backpack should be stowed in plastic bags. Take particular care that your billfold and fishing license are enclosed in one, and be sure to include your trout stamp if you are in a trout area. It is not at all unusual to wade out into water deep enough to wet the bottom of the pack before realizing it. Carry an extra plastic bag or two in case replacements are needed. On occasion I put my entire backpack and my clothes into an oversized trash bag to keep them dry so that I can swim a deep hole to explore something especially interesting on the other side. Inflated trash bags also make handy floats when I paddle across with all that gear.

Caution is in order for those of you who like to carry a camera along on your hikes. It is all too easy to ruin a roll of film or even your camera because of an overly long strap, so shorten it enough that you can just barely pull it over your head. Slip a heavy plastic freezer bag over the camera and up around the strap, securing it in place with a strong rubber band. The shortened strap enables you to carry the camera more comfortably, without as much bouncing, and makes it less likely to be damaged by being partially submerged should you stumble and fall. The plastic bag really wouldn't keep the camera dry if it were dunked completely under, since the bag isn't watertight where the strap passes through; but this arrangement does help ward off occasional splashes and keeps perspiration from fogging the viewfinder, which can lead to moisture working its way into the camera's interior. Ordinary leather or plastic cases are simply not enough protection from the water.

Use sunscreen liberally, renewing it every four hours, even when the sun isn't shining. Possibly as a consequence of problems with the ozone layer, the danger of skin cancer seems to get greater every year. Even if you already have a tan and aren't afraid of burning, sunscreen keeps the sun from sapping your strength on hot summer days; I always feel much fresher at the end of the day when I have used these lotions as I should. Polarized sunglasses capable of deflecting ultraviolet rays will not only protect your eyes, they will allow you to see beneath the surface of the water more easily.

If you haven't fished small streams before, remember that the most important factor in such waters is stealth— move very slowly and be absolutely quiet. Use small baits and a light line, and if at all possible, avoid letting your shadow fall across a spot you plan to fish. Don't pass up small pockets that are just marginally deeper than the narrow runs they border because large fish can hide in the most unlikely places. Use lures that have single hooks with the barbs depressed or filed off so you can more easily release fish unharmed. Barbless hooks come out of your hide more easily too. Keep your line taut while landing fish and very few will be lost because the barbs have been removed.

Don't be concerned about taking short trips away from the stream when you are far away from farms and houses, unless you see posted signs. Most landowners in this part of the Ozarks are not bothered by hikers or fishermen passing unobtrusively through outlying portions of their land. The possible exception may be someone from another area who has recently purchased property here. Practically every owner I have met along the streams in over thirty years of hiking has stopped to have a friendly talk with me about how my fishing was going. It is rare to find someone who is not friendly unless he has had repeated problems with vandalism.

Stay within the high-water banks of the stream when you are near roads or other signs of habitation. Even an Ozark farmer would become upset at someone walking across his lawn or through his barnyard without first asking permission. Obviously, you shouldn't violate no-trespassing signs; intruding upon posted land is sure to result in an unhappy landowner and a less than pleasant reception for hikers who come along later. Show a little consideration for the rights of the property owner and you will usually be well received. In each chapter I attempt to list the places where you should ask permission and those that you should avoid setting foot on at all costs. A little forethought can save some severe headaches.

I have read in Leonard Hall's *Stars Upstream* of the pitiable state that populations of beaver, turkey, and deer had sunk to along the Current and Jacks Fork in the mid-1950s. Many of the areas I describe in this book are near

or along the headwaters of these rivers, and it is a pleasure to observe that the situation is much better today.
Due to wise conservation practices, game laws, extensive
restocking, and a more informed public, these species
and others have made a marvelous comeback in the last
thirty years. Regrowth of forests along the rivers in the
National Scenic Riverways system of the Park Service
has played a big part in this recovery, as has the enlight-
ened Forest Service management of the extensive wood-
lands within the Mark Twain National Forests.

It is true, however, that use of the larger sections of the
rivers has increased with every passing year. They are so
crowded with canoes and inner tubes in the spring and
summer, all the way through Labor Day, that I avoid them
at all costs during those times. The tourist influx on the
larger streams is no small part of the reason for my love of
the remote, quiet places I describe in this book. I am not
afraid, on the other hand, that my haven of secluded
streams will suffer a similar invasion, because only those
willing to expend considerable effort will ever experience the beauty to be uncovered there.

For those who already love the quiet and peace of isolated areas, I hope this book will suggest new horizons.
For those who have not yet sampled such rare places, I
hope to plant seeds of desire that will turn them into
caretakers for an ancient and little-appreciated resource.

MAP 1

Sinking Creek

(Chapters 1–2)

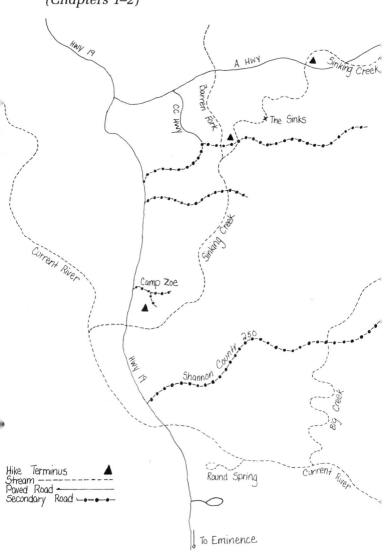

1

UPPER SINKING CREEK ═══════
(Map 1)

Sinking Creek is a wonderful little smallmouth stream that flows into the Current River a short distance upriver from Round Spring. Its odd name refers to an unusual feature of the creek that is one of the most improbable things you will ever see on any stream. In times of high water, part of the upper creek runs below a high cliff for several hundred yards before vanishing beneath its base in a huge, twisting whirlpool. Some of the older natives of the area insist that the creek's name should be "Sink In" Creek because it sinks into the rock face and disappears from sight. All the maps I have seen and the signs on the Highway 19 bridge, however, stick to the name "Sinking" Creek. Either way, it is a treat to hike the creek and discover the cause of its mysterious vanishing act. The creek is long and it is impossible to take it all in with a one-way hike to a second vehicle because of its unusual flow. It is best to take the upper, shorter portion of the hike first because you get the best view and full impact of the spot called "The Sinks" from that direction.

The upstream end of the hike is reached by taking Highway 19 north from Eminence for about twenty miles to A Highway. Follow A Highway east to the third bridge, the first with an appreciable flow of water from north to south under the highway. There are many parking spots on either side of the bridge over Sinking Creek. The stream is small here, but more than a little attractive. Immediately below the bridge it tumbles over a series of small ledges in some miniature falls before smoothing out into a long, quiet run for a quarter of a mile.

Walk in along the bottom of the ridge to the left, staying back from the creek to avoid extensive patches of poison ivy, and you will come to one of the attractions of the hike before you have done much more than get started. About one hundred yards downstream, Cave Spring Cave opens its eight-foot-high entrance amid a thick stand of trees at the base of the ridge. (I have my doubts about this name, but that is what is printed on the contour maps.) The cave consists of one large room thirty or forty feet deep that angles back to the right and then bears to the left at some small ledges. There is no spring issuing from this cave, but there is a sizable cold spring flowing from a much larger, deeper cave some three miles downstream. This cave is not named on my maps, and I suspect there has been a mix-up so that the name Cave Spring Cave actually belongs to the lower cave.

There are some surprisingly deep spots in this first part of Sinking Creek where you don't normally expect to find them. They lie along the sides of straight flows where there are no curves or boulders to cause uneven scouring of the streambed. Fish these little pockets carefully. A small bluff borders the left of the creek below the first cave, and a little cabin stands on the right a little farther down. Two fences only a few yards apart cross the creek in front of the cabin. Don't bother climbing over them, because they stop after crossing over to the gravel bar on the left. There they are joined, boxing in a small portion of the streambed. The fences aren't posted, but it is much easier to ford the creek and go around than to cross them.

Sinking Creek now winds back and forth gently for several hundred yards in an area where you may not notice many fish, but if you fish carefully and quietly, you can make better catches here than you might think. The first really big curve on the creek is a long, gentle swing to the left. You can make your walking easier and save time by cutting across the gravel bar on that side. There is little reason to stay on the stream here because it usually contains no deep water that could offer hiding places for fish.

You can continue down a field on the left until the road ends, intersecting the creek above a spot where a three-wire service line crosses overhead. There is a nice hole on the left past those lines where the creek sweeps to the right in a turn that skirts a wide, overgrown gravel bar. A small tributary flows in along the base of the ridge beyond the bar. It enters Sinking Creek about halfway down the long, straight flow past the curve.

Below the mouth of the tributary, a house sits back in the woods on the right. A little farther down is a private low-water bridge across the creek where a road extends to other buildings farther back against the hill. The hole below the bridge is usually full of smallmouth and isn't fished very often. I caught and released four keepers from this hole on my last hike. Every fish I caught was followed in by three or four others, each trying to snatch my lure from its mouth. The fenced land here is posted; stay in the streambed.

There is a sharp curve to the left past the bridge, with a fence crossing the creek in the middle of its shallow flow. Big cables tangled in driftwood are evidence that some more formidable barrier crossed the water in the past. Around the curve you will come upon a propane bottle on the edge of the field. It powers a pump that pulls water from the creek through a long pipe leading up the left bank.

After a swing to the east, beyond the end of a long straight run, there is an open field on the north. Behind the wooded bank on the south, another pasture runs away toward the next ridge. Ahead of you, at the far end of the field on the right, you can see a house and a barn with corrals for horses. The stream hits a beautiful stained bluff below the house and angles away to the left. There is excellent fishing water all along the base of the sheer rock cliff.

A faint road parallels the left side of the creek below the bluff. It runs on the creek side of a fence that borders a long field and soon crosses over to the right bank along another pasture. The road eventually returns to the left bank where yet another field begins above a thin line of trees.

Hiking downstream along the road saves some time, but this entire hike is short and you will miss a remarkable sight unless you hike back up the creek from the point the road first crosses from the left to the right bank. Ford the stream and walk upstream on the far bank until you come to a small spring branch that tumbles from the mouth of an extraordinary cave. This cave's entrance is some twenty-five feet wide and fifteen feet high and it gradually narrows to about four feet in width and seven feet in height at the back of the main room.

Nearly every cave I have found that has such a large entrance ends after it goes back thirty yards or less. Not this one! After the cave lowers and narrows, the passage bends to the right and continues essentially unchanged for another hundred feet, with the icy little stream flowing to mid-calf along its course. The floor of the cave then rises twelve to fourteen inches at a little ledge, over which the water drops in a noisy little fall. This rise of the cave floor cuts the vertical clearance a good deal and you would have to stoop to walk past that point. Although there doesn't seem to be anything in sight within the beam of my flashlight that would make it hard to go even farther into the hillside, I haven't explored beyond this ledge.

Watch where you step in this or any cave you enter and take care not to accidentally touch any of the sensitive formations that may be found there. The creations that took eons to form can be defiled or destroyed in a thoughtless instant. We have a responsibility to leave such things as much like we found them as possible, permitting others to view these wonders without a sign of our passing to mar the scene.

It's not a good idea to explore deep within a cave if you are alone, but this one could prove to be an interesting adventure for those well enough prepared to find out what lies beyond the little waterfall. This cave is the one I mentioned earlier that seems much more deserving of the name Cave Spring Cave than does the dry cave upstream.

Downstream from the next crossing, where the little road moves again to the left bank, an impressive bluff rises on the right. The creek turns slightly to flow along its base. The face of the bluff gradually steepens into a beautiful vertical cliff that soars to one hundred fifty feet above the streambed. Sinking Creek obediently runs along the cliff for a few more yards, and suddenly, without any warning of unusual things to come, the water of the stream does its improbable trick.

In an area of several small cave openings and strangely weathered rock formations, the stream vanishes with a sharp right turn into the gaping mouth of a tunnel some forty feet wide. The gracefully arching roof of the cave has a clearance of eight to ten feet over normal water level. The stream flows in misty green twilight completely through the ridge to emerge from the other side through an opening much like the one on the upstream end. The exit pool downstream is much larger and deeper than the pool at the entrance, making it very hard to get close to the tunnel from that direction. From its pool, Sinking Creek splashes smugly away toward the Current River, as if flowing through a solid rock wall is the most natural thing in the world for a little Ozark stream to do.

Uncounted years ago Sinking Creek flowed around the end of this ridge in an elongated bend. With the passing of time, the gradual weathering of the limestone in the cliff by acidic groundwater at the location of the present tunnel formed a small cave that finally pierced the ridge from one side to the other. Seeking the most direct path downstream, the stream poured through the cave, gradually enlarging it to its present size.

The old streambed around the ridge has been dammed to form two pretty lakes that lie across the gravel road past the end of the ridge. A third, smaller lake north of the road and close by the creek has been created by a dike that rises near the downstream end of the tunnel. This little lake is kept in an unattractive, muddy state by drainage from the road.

This area, called "The Sinks," was formerly run as a privately owned commercial venture offering boat rides through the tunnel. An extensive developed campground was built, running three quarters of a mile downstream along the gravel road to the low-water bridge across the creek on CC Highway. The decaying ruins of the tables and buildings of the campground are visible through the thickening undergrowth to those who drive by on the road.

The land along the creek here is posted against trespassing. Stay in the streambed and do not climb over the ridge to see the other side of the tunnel and the campgrounds. Those can be seen by coming upstream from the second low-water bridge on the gravel road past the end of CC Highway. CC Highway turns off A Highway a short distance after it leaves Highway 19. Another way for the more energetic to reach The Sinks from below is the hike up from the Highway 19 bridge that will be described in the next chapter.

Don't try to go through the tunnel. It is too dangerous. In high water the opening is not even visible as the creek disappears into the cliff face in a huge, swirling whirlpool. The sight of the stream twisting its way into such a vortex as it was "sinking" into the ridge during a minor flood is what led to the name Sinking Creek.

In low water the tunnel opening has plenty of clearance and the dark green water within is an eerie sight that draws you deeper inside. The tunnel seems deceptively short, with a small downstream exit, but this is because it dips down about halfway through the ridge until it has only a two-foot clearance above normal water level. The unknowing often interpret this low point as the end of the creek's shortcut through the ridge. Actually, the exit arch is much the same size as the upstream entrance and the tunnel is about two hundred feet long.

Remember, the water in the pool at the downstream end is very deep and very wide. Swimming through the ridge is not a good idea, even when water levels are down.

Take plenty of pictures. You will want them to help you remember the beauty of this spot. This hike is short and the fishing is good. Enjoy a leisurely trip upstream and return most or all of your catch for another hike on another day.

2

SINKING CREEK ━━━━━━━━━

Highway 19 to the Sinks
(Map 1, p. 10)

The hike up the lower part of Sinking Creek is about twice the length of the hike down to The Sinks from A Highway. In spots the scenery is memorable and the fishing is usually terrific. If you want to make this a one-way hike because of the length, a car can be left past the end of the blacktop on CC highway at the second low-water bridge. CC is the first hard-surfaced road leading to the right off A Highway, which begins twenty miles north of Eminence on Highway 19. The only parking spot here is to the left of the bridge as you approach from the west.

The downstream end of the tunnel at The Sinks lies three quarters of a mile upstream of this spot, around the long curve to the right. If you only want to see this end of the creek's plunge through the ridge and aren't interested in the rest of the hike, park here and take the compara-tively short trip upstream and back. Please remember that the land along the creek at the old campground to your right is posted against trespassing.

To reach the lower end of the longer hike, drive north on Highway 19 from Eminence to the first bridge beyond the Current River at Round Spring. Turn down the side road at the sign for Camp Zoe Campgrounds on the northwest side of the bridge. Follow it down under the bridge to the bars along Sinking Creek. There are many spots to park and a few developed camping areas.

Pay attention to the sign warning that the area is subject to flash flooding. If thunderstorms are in the forecast, don't park near water level—go back and park uphill along the side of the road that parallels the bridge. As along any Ozark creek, flash flooding from storms can be dangerous to the unwary, but if you are alert and prepared to move to higher ground at the first sign of rising water, rainy weather should not necessarily postpone your trip. With proper rain gear, a hike in the rain is an enjoyable experience.

A high, tree-covered bluff borders the creek on the right above the bridge, exhibiting an attractive, weathered surface covered with knobs and ledges. A small cave lies twenty feet up the bank from the upper end of the bluff, its head-high entrance screened by greenery in season. It is easy to miss if you don't search the rock surface carefully as you go by. There are many small openings farther along the bank, and patches of scouring rushes grow low against the water below the cave.

Portions of the campground border the water on the left. Tables and cleared picnic spots are visible through the trees along the stream before and along the big curve ahead. There is deep water both upstream and downstream of this bend where swimmers will often be found in warm weather. Surprisingly, the fish seem to have gotten used to people splashing around in the water, and I almost always catch some good smallmouth from this part of the creek. I even caught a fourteen-inch fish from the upper pool one August day while a man, his wife, and his two young boys were in the water nearby. The father was sympathizing with me because he was afraid his family's noisy play was scaring away the fish, when the smallmouth struck and tried to get away by heading for his legs. The memory of his frantic dancing as he tried to avoid the darting fish still makes me smile.

A spring flows in from the right as you round the next

bend. This spring is in the cleared area where you see the developed land and stables of Camp Zoe. This is a private area for paying guests. Stay within the boundaries of the stream throughout this straight run and around the curve at the end of the large gravel bar above. The main entrance to this camp is off a gravel road that intersects Highway 19 from the east between Sinking Creek and the Current River.

Deep water borders the eighty-foot bluff across from Camp Zoe and continues around the curve that begins after the bluff fades to a wooded ridge. On my last trip up the creek, a magnificent ten-point buck, with its half-grown antlers encased in a thick coat of velvet, crossed less than fifty yards ahead of me on this bend. He was clambering up the ridge and was already out of sight before I could get over my surprise, close my mouth, and focus my camera on him. An alert person could get many more good wildlife pictures than I have taken on my hikes, but I have had immeasurable fun getting the ones that I have.

After you pass through a long, swift section of the creek, a cliff with a vertical drop of about sixty feet rises along the left bank. Its upper end has a truly unique doubly curving face that sweeps out over the water in a setting that would be a landscape artist's delight. There is deep water directly beneath the foot of the cliff and for a short distance upstream.

Take a shortcut across the bar that runs past the cliff on the right bank. This is quicker than walking along the swiftly flowing riffles of the shallow, winding stream. Go up the dry channel that runs along the edge of the gravel bar near the trees. It comes out of the willows at the base of the next ridge where the creek straightens out and splits around another bar. The riffles up the right side of this little gravel island are especially pretty.

Ahead, around a brief left bend, Sinking Creek winds easily through long shallow runs toward the ridge ahead. As you approach the ridge, there is a series of overhanging ledges low against the water on the right where I have come across some of the biggest soft-shell turtles I have ever seen. Soft-shell turtles are extremely flat and have a long neck and a head tipped with a narrow, elongated snout, making them impossible to confuse with any other turtle. On the back side of the curve that begins beyond these ledges is a swampy area that sports an attractive stand of tall rose mallows. The flowers rise nearly seven feet when mature, and if you are there when they are blooming, you will see that they are the less-common pink variety of these large members of the hibiscus family.

Stay on the bar to the right, bypassing some marginally deep water, until it ends in one of the largest pools on the creek. I have caught smallmouth here up to eighteen inches in length. The best fish seem to congregate near the upper end of the hole along the right bank. There is a rock face that rises to eighty feet or more back in the trees beyond this deep pool. It is hard to see in spring and summer because of the thick leaves. Spring and summer are usually better for fishing and viewing wildflowers, but fall or winter hiking will reveal many features on the slopes that are hidden in the warmer seasons. I have had consistent success fishing the four-to-five-feet-deep areas along the banks on this part of the creek. The best spots seem to be in the shadier nooks and in places with a slight riffle in the water around large rocks and fallen logs. Beyond a faint road that cuts across the stream, there is a good-sized cave mouth up high on a bluff that rises before the creek rounds a slight turn to the left. The cave is virtually inaccessible without climbing equipment.

Soon you will come to a long, flowing hole where the creek moves away from the ridge to a rock face twenty feet high. An ancient cedar that has been broken and twisted by time crowns the little bluff. The gnarled old tree looks down on a nice pool at the base of the rock. The pointed aspect of a high ridge is visible in the distance straight up the valley.

After half a mile of gentle curves and swift, shallow runs, the creek swings in a long bend to the right along that ridge. A round cave mouth yawns thirty feet up the rock face where the cliff becomes barer and steeper. A heavy growth of ferns below the cave indicates a persistent flow of water, even in the dry times of late summer. There are long stretches of deep water along the bluff side of the creek across from a wide bar. I have caught smallmouth up to nineteen inches long around the boulders and logs of these pools.

A road comes in at an angle from the left a hundred yards before the creek turns along a forty-foot bluff. At its base there are intermittent spots of deep water for several hundred yards. As the deep holes give way to swift rapids and splashing rills, the creek swings back and forth over occasional sheets of limestone to another beautiful pool on a curve to the right. A neatly trimmed lawn leads up from the left bank to a private house that overlooks this pretty section of Sinking Creek. Another road crosses from the left before the end of the next bar.

Shallow and swift after a small turn to the left, the stream moves back and forth between low bluffs on either side of the valley. Power lines cross overhead beyond a sharp bend along a large hay field on the right bank, and you can see ahead to the first of the low-water bridges over the creek. This one would be more appropriately referred to as a concrete ford, since there are no culverts and all the water pours over the roadbed. The road that crosses here leads back to Highway 19 on the left. It dead-ends in the other direction past several houses and trailers along a little spring branch that enters a few yards upstream of the ford.

There is little deep water above this point until you come to a pool on the left with a house close above it. This house is on a small county road that parallels the creek for a short distance. More houses and buildings are visible through the trees as you go farther upstream. The road soon angles away to make its way around a larger tributary of Sinking Creek that comes in straight down the valley ahead of you.

The Barren Fork enters from the north above a large patch of cane that is the tallest and thickest I have seen this side of a southern swamp. Sadly, the cane is on a high dirt bank that is eroding away on the outside of a curve. This entire patch will probably be washed away before too many years have gone by.

Contour maps indicate several caves along the divide between the Barren Fork and Sinking Creek. Farther upstream, some big springs are shown flowing into the Barren Fork. I have meant to hike up to these caves and springs for years, but have always been sidetracked by the fishing and scenery on the main stream. One of these days. . . . Oh well! Maybe you'll beat me to it.

Sinking Creek winds back and forth above the Barren Fork with a noticeably reduced flow. It comes up against the base of a two-hundred-foot ridge at a twenty-five-foot rock front and gradually bends left at a pool of green water. The creek straightens out toward the low-water bridge on the gravel road at the end of CC Highway near The Sinks. I mentioned earlier that the land above this bridge at the old campground on the right is posted. The large signs attesting to the fact that the area is patrolled by the Shannon County Sheriff's Department seem highly convincing, but I smiled when I first saw them. Shannon County is a large, sprawling county that is sparsely settled, and it is hard to get to many spots because of extensive wilderness and poor roads. At present there are only two members of the Sheriff's Department to do the patrolling.

It is sad to look across the nearly mile-long campground and think of the wasted effort and resources that went into making this area a popular tourist attraction. Almost everything is now rotted away beyond repair, even the split-rail fences, many of which were made of valuable native walnut. The exact reason for the spot being closed is hard to imagine. It would seem to me that with good advertising this beautiful place would have drawn crowds of visitors.

Sinking Creek makes a long, gradual curve lined with deep pools as it passes by the campground. A half mile upstream it fronts a bluff that is crowned by an impressive rock face leaning far out over the creek nearly one hundred feet above the water. The stream sweeps away from this cliff and then bends sharply left into the big hole through the ridge at the west end of The Sinks.

If you have been to the upper end, you will see that this exit opening is as large or larger than the entrance. It is not possible to wade up and look through from this end as you can on the other side—the water is too deep and the pool too wide. The levee to your right as you face the tunnel is the last of the dams across the old channel that was cut off when the creek took its marvelous detour. It backs up a small lake on this side of the gravel road along the edge of the old campgrounds. Two much larger and clearer lakes lie in the old streambed across the gravel road that runs by the campground.

Take plenty of pictures of The Sinks before you start back down to whichever spot you have chosen to end your hike; this indescribable feature must be seen to be believed.

MAP 2

Big Creek Northeast of Eminence

(Chapter 3)

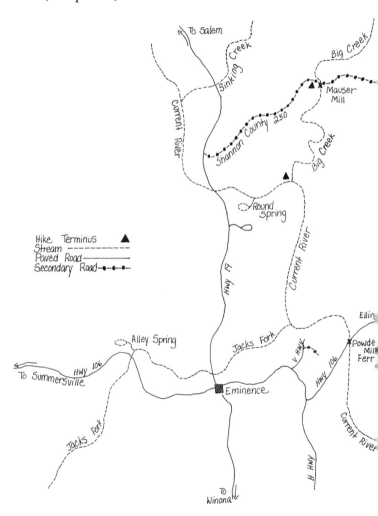

3

BIG CREEK
NORTHEAST OF EMINENCE ═══════

Mauser Mill to the Current River
(Map 2)

This stream, the easternmost of two long creeks in this book that are appropriately named Big Creek, flows in a general southwesterly direction from a point south of Bunker along the Dent-Shannon County line to the Current River five miles east of the Highway 19 bridge. For a hike on the lower section of the creek, drive north from Eminence on Highway 19 to Round Spring and the Current River.

As you drive up the highway, look for the short length of virgin pine forest that surrounds the roadbed about two miles north of the intersection of D Highway. The pines border the highway for two hundred feet on both sides of the center line. The area is clearly marked with large signs on the roadside, and it is kept attractive and well groomed in memory of the large stands of pine that covered this region before the intensive logging operations stripped the hillsides many years ago.

When you reach the sign to Round Spring just before the Current River bridge, pull into the parking area and take a few moments to visit this unusual feature. It can be seen in fifteen minutes from the time you turn off the highway, but the beauty of the spot will probably hold you longer.

The spring partially fills a circular depression some one hundred feet across that was formed when the roof of an ancient cave collapsed. Its beautiful blue water flows out of the pool under the south rim through a natural tunnel that is the last remnant of the cave. From the old cave mouth the spring branch runs out under a footbridge to join the Current River a short distance away. Muskrats are becoming more common here, and it is not unusual to see one feeding on the vegetation in the spring flow.

There is a large, impressive cave on the other side of Highway 19 in the same valley as the spring. Follow the signs along the paved road that crosses under the highway bridge. After reading about the cave on the bulletin board at the parking area on the west end of the road, you might be interested in taking a tour. It is managed by the U.S. Park Service and tours are given for a small fee several times a day during the season.

From Round Spring continue driving north on Highway 19 across the Current River until you pass under large power lines. Take the first county road that turns to the right past these lines. This is Shannon County 250, which you should follow for seven miles to the low-water bridge over Big Creek. Along the way you will pass through three small streams that flow across the road at gravel fords. Of course, these crossings can be quite dangerous in rainy weather, and I would recommend a vehicle with greater traction and clearance than an ordinary passenger car on this road. Many local people do use ordinary cars on this and other roads like it, but particular care must be taken in fording the creeks. It is easy to get stuck by going too slowly through them or to have large rocks damage the undercarriage of a low-slung car.

There are several parking spots on both sides of the bridge over Big Creek at Mauser Mill. Be careful about parking in the very loose gravel on the bars. It is extremely easy to get stuck in them if you are in a two-wheel-drive vehicle.

The hike down this section of the creek is somewhat longer than most described in this book. It takes over four hours of rapid walking to get to the mouth of the creek at the Current River. If you take the normal amount of time for sight-seeing or fishing, it could take six hours or more for the one-way trip downstream. Of necessity, you must retrace your steps on this hike because there is no way to get an ordinary vehicle to the lower sections of the creek. If you take this hike, judge your time and your endurance carefully and start back when either is running low.

The hike begins below the low-water bridge at Mauser Mill in a long, shallow section of the stream. You will pass a house trailer that sits above you on the high bank to the left, and soon your way will be blocked by a barrier of sheet metal and treated lumber that is strung across the channel on heavy cables. This barrier and one farther downstream utilize the best idea I have ever seen to effectively fence in a streambed with something that won't be torn up or swept away in high water. In low water it is quite easy to squeeze under and continue on your way.

Below this point there are some pretty rapids and a nice pool along the pasture to the right. Across the field you can see the small cabin and barn that you passed earlier as you came in on the county road. Past the field there is a splashing run where the creek bubbles over small ledges and gray boulders. It then bears left along a two-hundred-foot-high wooded ridge after Mash Creek adds its small volume to the flow. Mash Creek is the last stream you drove across before you came to the low-water bridge over Big Creek. The curve below Mash Creek is a long oxbow that has scattered deep holes along its outer perimeter close against the base of the ridge.

If you want to shorten the hike a little, there is a trail you can follow along the fence that cuts straight through the edge of the woods across the neck of this meander. Be careful if you take this shortcut. There is a lot of old fencing, both woven and barbed wire, lying all along the trail. A shagbark hickory stands close against the trail where it veers back down to the gravel bar along the creek. Look for an eighteen-inch-thick tree with compound leaves that seems to be shedding its bark in long, peeling strips. Near the spot at which the trail rejoins the creek, there is another barrier similar to the one upstream.

Around a ninety-degree bend to the right, Big Creek hits a small bluff that is weathered and carved into all sorts of wonderful shapes. Cross over above the bluff and get on the right side. There is some deep water around the large boulders in the pool at the foot of the ridge. Beyond this point the creek flows through a long, fairly straight run of shallow water for three-fourths of a mile. Another of the many high ridges that dominate the area cuts across the creek downstream beyond a gentle bend. There is a wide bar on the inside of the next big curve to the left, but there would be no time saved in cutting across the bar because the creek swings back to the right again in a few hundred yards. Well downstream the creek's flow quickens and curves into a wide, deep pool before it hits a rock bluff straight on and is deflected to the left. There is little water of any appreciable depth for a long distance beyond this bend.

The ridges are very high and impressive around the Big Creek watershed, and their looming presence at the end of every turn of the valley adds much to the atmosphere of this hike. Contour maps show that the ridgetops are three hundred feet and more above creek level. The valley meanders gradually back and forth toward one ridge and then another until a large slough enters from the right along the rocky face of a wooded slope. Its water is still and murky with overgrown, swampy banks. This is one of the few places I have seen cottonmouths along Big Creek. They are not common, though many people panic and think they are seeing one when they encounter a dark snake of any variety. But you should still be careful in this spot if you decide to stray from the gravel bar.

One hundred yards from the next ridge a spring branch comes in from the left. It is a considerable distance back up the little creek to the spring, but it is an interesting hike in seasons when the banks are not too overgrown. A quarter of a mile farther down you will come to a small bluff that is made especially attractive by the intimate nature of the spot. Its beauty is emphasized by the small size of the creek and your closeness to the rock front when you are standing near the bank. The water here is over waist deep even in summer.

Past this interesting rock formation there is an extensive gravel bar on a wide peninsula that is enclosed by a long curve to the left. A lofty ridge stands beyond the bend, some two hundred fifty feet above the valley floor. Taking the sharpest cutoff possible across the neck of the turn saves a great deal of walking and brings you out at a high bluff with considerable vegetation covering much of the exposed rock. One July I saw two deer crossing in a shallow riffle downstream from this bluff, and one of them stopped a few seconds to stare at me before it trotted casually on. I managed to snap one of my favorite wildlife photos while it was watching me. Interestingly, deer don't seem nearly as frightened at the sight of a person wading in a creek as they do when they see someone on the bank.

There is little deep water and no lofty bluffs along Big Creek to this point. The tall, wooded ridges and wide, sweeping curves are the main attraction so far. A gentle curve now sweeps to the right, and a short distance before the next ridge several large cedars border the creek at water level. Cedars are not uncommon along Ozark streams, but examples as big and old as these are rare. Ring studies have shown other cedars of this size to be up to seven hundred years old. Undercutting by floods is sure to wash these away in time, but for now they make an impressive sight. I have caught smallmouth below these trees on several hikes down Big Creek.

At the next bend, the creek is turned to the side by a moderately high bluff running from east to west. At its base lies the first really deep hole you will come across. On midsummer afternoons, the sun shines from the northwest across this pool, which reflects hypnotic patterns of light and shadow onto the rock wall opposite. Large fish are common in the green, shadowed depths, and longear sunfish spawn and guard their nests in the shallows through the end of July. As you hike past this pool, listen for the staccato call of pileated woodpeckers that often echoes through the hills all along the Current River watershed. This largest of North American woodpeckers sounds a little like Woody Woodpecker of the cartoons, and his crested red, white, and black plumage further empha- sizes the resemblance. The large size and jerky, uneven flight pattern make them easy to identify if you are lucky enough to see one pass overhead.

There is no more deep water until the creek strikes the next ridge, not even small pockets around boulders. Along the ridge is another deep pool beneath an area of exposed bedrock at the base of a small cliff. Soon an ATV track crosses the creek along a large bend to the left. Another high ridge is visible far ahead. You can cut across the bar on this curve to save time, but the water in the creek channel grows consistently deeper as you approach the Current River. It would be a good idea to stick to the stream if you still have the time for some fishing.

After a long rainbow of a curve, the creek runs directly against the high ridge ahead and follows it off to the left. There are more and more deep pools and high bluffs downstream, but this is approaching the limits of a nor- mal hike. There is no way for any vehicle to be waiting for you at the river unless you have someone who can pick you up in a boat by coming down from the Highway 19 bridge over the Current River.

Short of the next ridge, another ATV trail crosses diag- onally from the left after you pass a spring branch that enters from that side. You can follow the road back to the left for about ten minutes through thick woods to a large spring. The spring has a long, lily-pad-filled pool that lies against an overgrown rock outcropping. Except for the rocks, this place is so swampy and tropical-looking that it would seem more appropriate in the Deep South.

If you continue down to the river, turn upstream and look for the large cave mouth high on the river side of the

tall bluff that rises at the mouth of Big Creek. It is reported to pierce the ridge completely and come out in a
much smaller opening on the creek side of the prominence. The cave is far above the river, and I have never
braved the two narrow passages to the rear of the first
chamber to see if one of them does indeed tunnel all the
way through.

Keep track of the time you have taken to reach your
turnaround point, wherever you stop, and judge carefully when you should start back. Remember that you are
going to be more tired on the return hike and likely to be
walking more slowly.

MAP 3

Rocky Creek, Thorny Creek, and Prairie Hollow Creek

(Chapter 4)

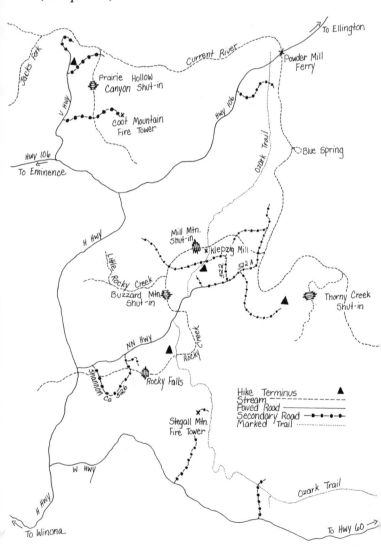

4

ROCKY CREEK ══════════════

Rocky Falls to the Current River
(Map 3)

No trip through the central Missouri Ozarks would be complete without a visit to Rocky Creek, a small tributary of the Current River in Shannon and Carter counties. Along this little stream and in nearby valleys, you will find five of the most scenic shut-in areas in the entire state. Shut-ins are unusual geologic features which result when a stream that has been running over comparatively soft sedimentary rock encounters harder igneous rock and flows right through the formation instead of going around it. In this region, the narrow, canyonlike channels which result have exposed extensive layers of red porphyry that are crowded with a chaotic jumble of boulders. This striking rock is closely related to granite in appearance and composition, and the variety found here exhibits varying colors ranging from subdued purples to light oranges and pinks. Several theories have been proposed to explain the formation of shut-ins, but regardless of their cause, they are often spectacular. These spots are more impressive in high water, but they are always eye-catching, even when water levels are low. Visit them at different seasons of the year and you will be amazed at their constantly changing aspect.

Not as well known as the more popular Johnson Shut-Ins in Reynolds County, these spots along the Carter-Shannon County line are every bit as attractive. The lack of crowds and the chance to enjoy the scenery at leisure make these smaller features a relaxing pleasure to visit. A turn-of-the-century grist mill at the lower end of Mill Mountain Shut-In makes it even more notable. The higher neighboring ridges are often topped with treeless glades that overlook miles of beautiful wooded valleys and hills that stretch away to the horizon. Parts of the Ozark Trail parallel the stream for several miles, and wildlife is plentiful throughout the area. Canoe trips on the Current River are offered at the nearby Two Rivers Campground.

Unless the water is high, fishing along Rocky Creek is limited to a few deep holes and the ponds created by beaver dams. In times of high water, some fish do migrate upstream from the Current River, and then you would be more likely to catch a few in the lower reaches of the creek. I occasionally take my ultralight spinning rod along on a hike down Rocky Creek, but fishing is not the main attraction—the scenery is.

To reach Rocky Falls, take U.S. 60 to Winona. Travel north on Highway 19 for less than a mile and then turn right on H Highway. Follow H for ten miles as it twists and turns in a gradual arc around to the north until its intersection with NN. Full of hills and curves, this stretch of highway is wonderfully scenic, but the drive will not be enjoyable for those prone to motion sickness.

Three valleys along H Highway have signs warning that the road could become impassable in high water. If it has been raining for long, the highway can be flooded. It would be dangerous to try driving through flowing water that comes as much as halfway up the tires of your car. I once came far too close to being swept off a low-water bridge when the water was barely up to the hubcaps of my full-sized pickup.

Turn right on NN and proceed two miles to the second intersection of NN and Shannon County Road 526, which leads to Rocky Falls. There is a small sign just before the turnoff indicating that the falls lie to the right. Take this well-tended road for a half mile to the falls, leaving 526 by bearing to the left when the road forks. At this point 526 loops back around to the east where it again intersects NN Highway. Some older books indicate that it is easy to confuse the correct road down to Rocky Falls with some old logging roads, but this isn't true any longer. The primary road has been widened recently, and a great deal of chat has been spread to improve its surface.

There is a large parking and picnic area right by the water at Rocky Falls. Make certain you have your camera with you and plan to spend a pleasant hour or two exploring and walking around the forty-foot-high shut-in. Not a true waterfall, the steep cascade is still so impressive that it brings people back time and time again. The easiest path downstream from the falls is on the side opposite the parking area along an old road that crosses the creek immediately below the large pool beneath the falls. If the water level is normal to low, you can step across on large rocks beside the roadbed. If the water is up, plan on getting a little wet.

Follow the dirt road north for about fifty yards and then cut across to the creek if you wish to walk along a beautiful bluff pool that is a favorite haunt of beavers. A twenty-foot cliff of black-coated rock rises sharply from the water along the west bank of the pool, and it makes an ideal spot to hide and watch the beavers in the water below. If you want to get some pictures of them, conceal yourself atop the bluff early in the morning or just before sunset. Be quiet and be patient.

Take care when walking near the lower bank of the pool on the east side. It is riddled with the rear entrances of beaver dens. My son Scott and I once had a beaver pop out of one of the tunnels directly between us as we stood by the pool one afternoon. Unfortunately, the beaver recovered its wits before we did, and it dove back into its den before I could get a photograph.

If you stick to the creek for the two miles down to its crossing of NN, you will usually find several beaver dams and ponds—unless high water has swept them away. Deer and turkey are also common in the Rocky Creek watershed, partly because of the nearby Peck Ranch Wildlife Area. Those hikers who walk quietly and are watchful stand a good chance of seeing beavers, deer, turkeys, and smaller wildlife in almost any season. If you want to make your hike a little easier, stay on the dirt road all the way to NN Highway. Keep an eye on the lower branches of the trees along your way. There are ordinarily many large hornet nests along this part of the creek. Unless a recent freeze has dulled the activity of the hornets, you want to avoid disturbing the nests at all costs. Believe me, they feel more strongly about their property than you do, and their protectiveness will bring painful stings to the unwary.

There is an interesting side trip leading away from the creek about a half mile below Rocky Falls, where a sign directing hikers to the falls indicates an intersection with the Ozark Trail. The trail is marked by small green and white signs with a vertically overlapping *O* and *T*. Two miles to the right up the Ozark Trail and about four hundred feet higher in elevation, the Ozark Trail reaches the top of Stegall Mountain. The course of the trail across the bare top of the mountain is marked by a series of cairns (small piles of stones), since there aren't any trees growing there to put the trail signs on. The mountaintop is a bald glade littered with large outcroppings of the same type of red porphyry found in the shut-ins, and the view in all directions is impressive. If there is not too much haze, you can see eastward all the way to Taum Sauk Mountain, the highest point in Missouri.

A few yards before you reach the mountaintop, the trail intersects an old dirt road that leads to the Stegall Mountain fire tower, about a mile to the right. The top of the tower is kept locked, but as of this writing you can still climb up and enjoy the view from the topmost flight of steps. If you take the time for a trip to the tower, you'll find the view even better than that from the open glade back down the trail.

When you reach Highway NN on your downstream hike, bear to the right (eastward) along the asphalt road and watch for the continuation of the small green and white Ozark Trail signs that resume on the north side of the roadbed about fifty yards east of the bridge over Rocky Creek. The trail is rather winding here, turning well away from the creek, but the going is much easier than on the stream bank. I usually stay on the stream, however, since there are several small pools in this area that may contain a fish or two.

Half a mile farther downstream, at a spot where the Ozark Trail twists back to the stream through a maze of giant red porphyry boulders, Rocky Creek fights its way through a second shut-in. Here a shoulder of Buzzard Mountain intrudes upon the creek from the west and creates a steep series of rapids and small falls which splash through a narrow defile that it is hard to tear yourself away from. This shut-in is smaller than Rocky Falls, but the rock is more jumbled and the colors are much brighter.

After you pass Buzzard Mountain Shut-in, the Ozark Trail gradually veers away from the creek, taking a more direct route across a long curve to Mill Mountain Shut-in and Klepzig Mill, about a mile and a half away. The stream itself has few pools in this area, but you might want to follow it down to its intersection with Little Rocky Creek for another side trip.

This small feeder stream enters from the west as the main stream swings back sharply to the right to run almost due east. The going is difficult along the smaller creek because of thick undergrowth, but there is a much easier path up the valley along an old abandoned road that runs through the woods on the far side of the field to the north. Old concrete bridges, crumbling to ruin along the disused road, reveal that this was once a well-traveled route. If you take the road upstream to the northwest, go over to the stream frequently. There are small bluffs and springs all along its flow, and even a beaver pond or two worth seeing.

Buzzard Mountain, to the south of Little Rocky Creek, rises some four hundred feet above the valley floor and offers fabulous views from its open summit. Like Stegall Mountain, it is littered with porphyry boulders and ledges, and from its northwest prominence you can see all along Little Rocky Creek Valley.

Take the road north of the creek far enough and you will find that it swings straight across the top of the meadow and into the edge of the woods. There it turns back in a more westerly direction and intersects the creek. The road crosses the stream twice within a half mile and passes near several houses. After the second crossing, stay on the north side of the creek and keep an eye out for a sinkhole next to a small ravine. Sinkholes are circular depressions of varying sizes that are formed when the roofs of ancient caves collapsed. On one side of this one, in an unusual geologic feature, a tunnel leads completely through the border of the sinkhole to the side of the nearby ravine.

About a half mile below the mouth of Little Rocky Creek, at the point where the Ozark Trail again crosses the main creek, the valley narrows once more and the waters rush through the beautiful Mill Mountain Shut-in. At the downstream end of the shut-in stands the structure responsible for its name: Klepzig Mill. Be ready to spend more time here taking photographs, exploring, and simply enjoying yourself.

The old grist mill was built prior to 1912, and the crumbling concrete ruins above it testify to the ingenuity and energy of the builders. The existing partial dam once extended completely across the creek, forming a large pool. It controlled and diverted the flow of Rocky Creek so it could be used to power the mill machinery. An elderly gentleman I met near the mill one March day told me that when he was a boy the pool above the dam was a popular swimming hole.

Water could be released through a gate in the dam and funneled through a concrete flume along the south side of the creek where it dropped into a large concrete well, turning a horizontally mounted turbine before rejoining the creek below the mill. The machinery was fitted with a generator in the early 1940s to transform the flow of water into electric power. A few yards above the mill is a small spring house where a cold spring still flows from a large clay tile. Kept cool by spring water, the chamber below the tile was used to store perishable goods in the time before electricity was available. Across the road from the mill, a little beyond the parking area, there are several large yews that indicate the position of an old house.

The Ozark Trail crosses the creek below Klepzig Mill and continues across the high ridge to the north. It dips through the valley of Indian Creek, an interrupted stream that has an occasional beaver pond along its course. Then the trail turns to follow the Current River along beautiful bluffs that tower up to two hundred feet above the river. The trail parallels the river to an access point below the old Powder Mill Ferry, which is across the river from Blue Spring. This area can also be reached by traveling east from Eminence on Highway 106 and turning to the right before reaching the bridge over the Current River.

Rocky Creek flows below the mill for another two miles to the river, between Barnett Mountain to the north and Mill Mountain to the south. For the first mile there is a large meadow beneath Mill Mountain, and the stream hugs the shoulder of Barnett Mountain against sheer bluffs. There are a few deep holes in this stretch that sometimes hold fish if water conditions are favorable.

The creek then passes through a small wooded section where a little road crosses at a gravel ford. A pasture opens up on the north side of the stream a hundred yards below the crossing. A half mile farther Rocky Creek enters the Current River. The river here sports a deep, wide run that has an impressive bluff at its lower end. There is a camp house clinging to the side of a steep hill at the mouth of the creek.

Before it reaches the river, the road along Rocky Creek crosses over to the south bank and circles back about two miles to NN, the highway to Rocky Falls. At the point the asphalt begins, another dirt road, Shannon County 522, leads off to the north and curves westward to parallel the creek after a few hundred yards. It will take you to Klepzig Mill after two miles of moderately rough driving. This narrow lane is graded regularly and is passable in most cars if you are alert to rocks, which often tumble down the hillside from the south and litter the road surface.

There are many roads that lead off into the hills in this area. Follow as many as you like, but be prepared to retrace your steps if you suddenly come across no-trespassing signs far back in the woods. The areas are posted primarily for hunters, but the owners of the property are usually nowhere near for you to ask permission to cross their land.

If you feel up to more rough hiking, there is another striking shut-in on Thorny Creek that you should visit. It lies completely around the huge downstream oxbow bend in the Current River below the mouth of Rocky Creek. Go downriver until you see the beautiful Cardareva Bluff towering high above the river on the other side. Thorny Creek enters the river on the west side, opposite the lower part of the bluff. Walk upstream on the creek for about a mile and the valley walls will close in steeply around you as the character of the rock in and around the streambed changes from sedimentary to igneous. Thorny Creek then splashes through the porphyry in another of the marvelous shut-ins that make this area so extraordinary.

You can get to Thorny Creek with a little less walking if you drive to the end of NN and keep going straight ahead on County Road 522–A. When it veers left just over a little creek, take the smaller road up the hill to the right. The road to the left goes over to the mouth of Rocky Creek. If the road is even a little muddy, I would suggest parking at the top of the hill around the first big curve to the left and walking the rest of the way. The next downslope is very steep and covered with slippery red clay.

After you cross the small streambed at the bottom of the first ridge, take the right fork in the road. Turn down the left branch of the road fifty yards ahead, and take the left branch again at the top of the first hill. There is a pond to the left near the bottom of the hill and another to the right after the fork at the top. You can sometimes see the Current River far below you through the trees to the left as you drop down into the first saddle atop the ridge.

Take the right fork after you pass the third saddle on the ridge crest. Continue to the right until you strike the little stream at the bottom of the slope. Follow it down to its junction with Thorny Creek. This is not as easy as it sounds because a tornado ripped its way through here a few years ago, and dead trees are scattered across your way for over a hundred yards. Walk up Thorny Creek a short distance to the shut-in.

The hike down from Rocky Falls to the Current River varies from six to seven miles, depending on your choice of routes. This could easily be covered in half a day, but given the side trips available and the distractions of the spectacular scenery, you could use the better part of two days and still feel like going back over parts of the hike again. Topographic maps would make finding your way through these desolate stretches much easier. The Rocky Creek and Thorny Creek shut-ins are included in the Powder Mill Ferry and Stegall Mountain 7.5–minute quadrangles. The maps are available from the Missouri Department of Natural Resources.

As long as you are in the area, there is another spot that you ought to visit. About ten miles to the northwest, in a small valley near the junction of Jacks Fork and the Current, lies Prairie Hollow Canyon, my favorite of all the shut-ins. To reach it, go back from Rocky Falls to H Highway and then north for four miles to Highway 106. Take 106 three miles west to V. Notice the sign at the intersection directing you to Two Rivers Campgrounds. Complete canoe trips of various lengths on both Jacks Fork and the Current are available there. V Highway can also be reached by going five miles east from Eminence on 106.

Follow V north for three miles until you see the sign that says you are entering Two Rivers Campgrounds. A short distance past this sign a small dirt road turns off to

the east. Pull in on this road and park to the right inside
the edge of the woods. An old, rusty sign indicates that
this is a private road, but this entire area is in the National Scenic Riverways, and the sign does not mean that
you can't park there. Don't try to drive down the old road
to the bottom of the hill to the east. It is very steep and
rough, and it doesn't lead to the canyon overlook.

Follow the nature trail indicated by the Park Service
sign on your left. If the trail is too faint to follow, as it
often is, simply go one-fourth of a mile straight east to
Prairie Hollow Canyon. After you see the first red porphyry
boulders, you have two ledges of the igneous rock to
clamber down, and then you are in the canyon proper.
Take some time while you climb around the top to ad-
mire the steep, narrow beauty of this marvelous little
gorge. It is easy to overestimate the depth of the narrow
canyon, but from the Eminence quadrangle map the contour lines show it to be some eighty to one hundred feet
deep.

Juneberries and redbuds filled the depths with splashes
of white and pink when I was there during a recent March,
and the songs of the little frogs known as "Spring Peep-
ers" echoed from the rocks so loudly that the sound was
almost overwhelming. Ferns thrive here in the moist air,
along with multicolored lichens and carpets of soft, green
moss. The canyon is beautiful in all seasons, but in early
spring, before the leaves return to the trees, the colors of
the rock are at their best and water levels are high. High
water makes the many waterfalls and rapids especially
impressive then, but whatever time you choose to visit
Prairie Hollow, you can't go wrong.

When you are ready to explore the bottom of the canyon, go upstream and follow the steeply slanting path
down to the creek. Across the canyon and upstream of
the point at which you reach the water, a small tributary
cascades over a series of small falls into the main stream.
As you near the creek on your way down, look between
the boulders; near the water a fissure going far beneath
the surface is worthy of being called a cave. To make your

tour a complete round-trip through the area, cross the stream below the wet-weather tributary falls and climb the far slope. Hike downstream on that side. The view to the bottom of the gorge from one of the ledges about fifty yards to the north is the most impressive of all.

I have read about a small arch somewhere on the east wall of the shut-in below the point you cross the creek, but I have not been able to verify its existence. One icy Sunday afternoon in November, I walked the canyon from one end to the other and could find no trace of an arch. The closest thing to one that I saw was a passage between two large boulders that had fallen against one another. By no stretch of the imagination could this be called an arch, but you might wish to hike and wade down the creek bed to see for yourself. There are several small caves scattered along both sides of the canyon that show evidence of water flowing from their mouths. Such features in igneous rock are a rarity and are deserving of close examination.

If you have taken the upper route downstream, continue on the east side until the canyon walls begin to level out and work your way back down to the creek. Cross over to the west bank and you will intersect a nature trail on that side. Follow it down to the primitive road that crosses Prairie Creek on a low-water bridge made of concrete. Take this road back up to the top of the hill on the west and you will be back at your starting point.

Be particularly careful when climbing and wading in this area and in any spot where there is danger of a fall resulting in severe injury; be even more cautious when hiking alone. Before visiting any of the unfrequented places I describe in this book, don't forget to inform someone of your planned route and time of return. Someone must know where to come looking for you if you become lost or injured.

MAP 4

Big Creek West of the Current River

(Chapters 5–7)

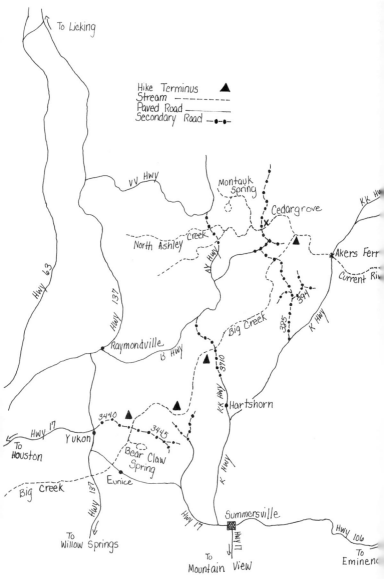

5

BIG CREEK ═══════════════

Upstream from County Road 3710
(Map 4)

This stream is the westernmost of two creeks with the same name that flow into the Current River within a few miles of one another. Big Creek runs south of Houston, under Highway 137 near Yukon, and into the Current about twenty miles north of Summersville. It flows through a scenic valley with areas of high bluffs that contain more caves than I have seen along any other stream in the Ozarks. Some of these caves are reported to go back long distances into the ridges. Many of them have impressively large entrances and bear evidence of use by fishermen and hunters as protected campsites.

Due to its length, Big Creek can't be hiked comfortably in less than three trips, and two of these are quite long. The first hike I describe is perhaps the most taxing, but it has extremely satisfying rewards waiting upstream for those patient enough to make their way through the long, dull lower reaches.

To reach the starting point, turn off U.S. Highway 60 east of Mountain View onto Highway 17 and go north a mile past Summersville to K Highway. Follow K to the junction where KK continues straight ahead and K veers to the right to its crossing of the Current River at Akers

Ferry. (This is one of the few remaining ferries still operating in the Ozarks. You might be interested in driving over to take a ferry ride before it too is taken out of commission.)

Continue north on KK to County Road 3710, which is simply an extension of KK after the hard-surfaced road ends. Follow the gravel road to its crossing of Big Creek on a concrete ford. Park to the left of the road before the sharp curve to the right that carries you on down to the creek. There are several spots where you can pull a vehicle off the road, but you should be careful not to park across the ATV tracks leading down to the gravel bars.

In the summer this portion of Big Creek is a long, wide gravel bar extending upstream for about five miles. The entire flow of the stream suddenly drops beneath the rocks below two beautiful pools far ahead of you and doesn't reappear until it is well past the point this hike begins. In rainy periods there are several stretches of deep water through here that have good fish populations, but due to increased water levels the creek is more difficult to hike and the trip will take longer than the one I describe. If you do decide to make the trip while the stream is flowing, plan carefully and remember that during most of the high-water period the season on black bass is closed for Missouri streams.

The wide, dry creek bed winds back and forth ahead of you, and there is an ATV road on the left at the first big bend. The road branches and one part goes over to the creek at the first curve to the right. Stay on the left branch, which returns to the streambed where a little valley enters from the right. I have seen deer all along the streambed for the next few miles, even when the creek is dry. Try to walk as quietly as possible and you will magnify your chances of seeing them.

In about a mile an electric line parallels the watercourse on the south through an overgrown field. A low rock face stands against the opposite bank as the channel swings in big curves through an extremely wide bar against the field. There is a private property sign on the bluff to the right; resist the temptation to explore that side.

Beyond the power lines follow the road going up the north bank among ridges that grow higher and steeper in the distance. Some are crowned with projecting rock outcroppings that are especially impressive in the winter. The road passes by an old barn along a dry tributary bed a short distance from the main creek, and there are tall bluffs visible to the right. Across the dry streambed the road goes by old fields thick with walnut trees.

At a sharp left turn in the road stands one of the most unusual trees I have ever seen. Someone or something twisted this odd, six-inch-diameter pine into a knot when it was smaller, and its trunk still turns incongruously through a full 360 degrees in a horizontal circle some four feet across. After completing the circle it straightens and grows upward normally as though it had done nothing out of the ordinary.

Up the next hill you will come to an ammonia pipeline right-of-way leading to the top of a ridge that rises over a hundred fifty feet above the valley floor. Deer and turkey are very common along the pipeline, and one July I saw over a dozen immature turkeys dusting themselves in the middle of the road near a small pond. At the top of the rise, this road intersects another dirt lane. If you turn left along this road, you will go back to KK, but you should turn right and follow it down to Big Creek.

This road branches at the bottom of the hill. Take the right fork across the streambed where it divides again. Stay to the left and this fork will take you back to the gravel bars. The road is not so well traveled and open in this section. ATV tracks and trails continue back and forth across the creek bed upstream. For easier walking, stay on the trails and watch carefully for their continuation on the opposite bank every time they intersect Big Creek.

There is an oddity that has developed over the years in this part of the streambed. Walk up the center of the dry channel for a while and you will find that you are sometimes going downhill in gradual drops of as much as twenty feet while you are still traveling upstream. These places are holes of considerable depth in high water, and their odd reverse slopes continue one after the other for almost two miles. The larger rocks, which make hiking slower and harder, are at the crests between the deeper areas of these dry pools. There is at least one small pool of water in a little cove of solid rock ledges some two miles below the mouth of Dry Bone Creek, the largest of the normally dry tributaries in this region of Big Creek.

After about five miles of walking, look for the mouth of Dry Bone Creek entering from the left. It comes in a few yards above a high bluff as the road crosses over to the left side of the main stream. What looks like a wide gravel road at the bluff's upstream end is actually the mouth of Dry Bone Creek. The road you are on continues up the left bank of Big Creek, but you will have to go up Dry Bone a few yards to find it.

Instead of immediately turning upstream on the main trail, walk along the road that goes up the smaller creek bed for a short distance. The side of the bluff opposite the main creek is more interesting than the Big Creek side. It is heavily weathered, with a few caves along its face, and after you have come such a long way without much notable scenery, the shaded recesses are a pleasant place to explore and relax a while.

Go on up the original road along the larger stream and follow it back and forth across the gravel beds while watching for a very high bluff on the left side of the creek. The spot where the flowing water disappears into the ground is a little downstream of the bluff. It runs briskly above this point through a shallow riffle that leads from a marvelous deep-green hole along the high rock face of the bluff. This steep precipice is accented with overhanging ledges and a very large cave mouth that opens midway up the cliff face.

The cave is not easily accessible. To get to it requires a swim across the extremely deep part of the pool or a difficult climb down from the hillside above. This pool is almost always a good fishing spot, and I usually spend a long time here taking full advantage of it. You deserve the chance to fish and relax by the cool, shaded water after such a long, dry hike.

A few hundred yards upstream, around a sharp bend to the right, you will come to another wonderful pool that is even longer than the one you just left. This hole is some two hundred fifty yards long and has very deep water at the upper and lower ends. An impressive rock prominence bulges into the stream before you get to the big bend at the upstream end. Deep water surrounds the rock on all sides and the entire pool from one end to the other consistently yields good fish. Fishing live crayfish on the bottom, I have caught several catfish from this pool and the one beneath the big cave.

There are alternating shallow runs and deep pools in the next mile of the creek once you hike beyond a long riffle in a steep, narrow valley. Although the creek above this point is worth seeing, there is no part if it for nearly two miles that can match the two large holes you have just passed. You have a hike of at least six miles ahead of you on your return trip if you go back downstream right now. It would be better to see the portions of Big Creek that lie farther upstream by walking down from Bear Claw Spring east of Yukon. Most of the caves along the creek lie in this region of beautiful cliffs and long stretches of deep water.

6

UPPER BIG CREEK ════════════════

Downstream from Bear Claw Spring
(Map 4, p. 46)

The county road to the upper part of Big Creek below Bear Claw Spring intersects Highway 137 twenty-five miles north of Willow Springs and eighteen miles south of Licking, at the little community of Yukon. This spot can also be reached by driving eight miles east of Houston on Highway 17. Turn east on County Road 3440, which is less than a hundred yards north of the intersection of Highways 17 and 137 at Yukon. Follow 3440 for two miles to the low-water bridge over Big Creek. Another route to Big Creek leads west for nine miles from Summersville to Eunice on Highway 17. Turn north on County Road 3445, bear left a few hundred yards later at the T intersection, and proceed for three miles to the creek.

Bear Claw Spring feeds into the creek from a point upstream of the parking area that is west of the bridge on 3440. Park here to see the spring and then cross over to the east bank of Big Creek. Turn to the left on the gravel road that runs beside the bars along the watercourse. Drive down the loose gravel of the road along the stream as far as the surface permits. After the water in the creek has been up, the gravel here can be very loose until it has been packed down by vehicles for a few weeks. If you have a truck or a four-wheel-drive vehicle, you can cross the creek at a gravel ford a quarter of a mile downstream. Then it is only a short distance to a parking area by a large swimming hole that lies at the base of a rugged bluff.

This pool is the only really deep water for a long distance in either direction. To save yourself an uninspiring trek, you can drive past this area along an even narrower track to a little turnaround short of the point it dead-ends in the stream. There is no place to park by the creek, so pull over uphill of the water in the small area to the left of the road. Parking here can keep you from getting stuck on the treacherous, sandy slope that leads down to creek level.

Walk along the road to the stream and your hike will take you through a gently curving, shallow section of the creek, which splashes downstream for several hundred yards toward a high ridge. Past the ridge the channel breaks out into an open area beyond four boulders. They lie in a narrow section of water where small, dark ledges border the stream under a low bluff. There is another small bluff on the left with a deep pool beneath it and an even prettier stretch of water farther downstream.

A faint road comes in on the left side below these long holes. Over the creek here stands a fifty-foot bluff with a bulging front that hangs out over deep, shaded water. Part of the road crosses the creek to the right. The other branch moves away from the creek and up the nearby ridge. Below this crossing the knee-deep creek is floored by flat sheets of slippery limestone for over one hundred fifty yards. These layers are followed by shallow, winding runs which empty into another pool that has limestone layers across only half its width.

There are many goggle-eye and longear sunfish in this part of the creek. Most people seem to catch them on live crayfish and minnows, and it is seldom hard to fill your stringer if you want to take home fish to eat.

In late summer you will notice occasional patches of

brilliant red Cardinal Flowers near the water's edge all along the creek. Their multiple blossoms crown a two-foot stalk, and the intense color of these lovely flowers adds an extra charm to an already attractive scene.

The creek now runs straight and narrow beside a gray, convoluted bluff which slopes down to a small cave that is sheltered beneath a jagged out-thrust of rock. Look carefully at the next rock outcropping on the right. Partially concealed from upstream and easy to miss as you walk down the creek is a small natural arch about ten feet high and twelve feet wide. The opening through the rock is about seven feet high and is best seen when viewed from slightly downstream. I made three trips down the creek before I noticed this unusual formation and was more than a little surprised when I found it.

Shallow and swift, Big Creek now runs straight until it turns ninety degrees to the right at a high, black-and-red-stained bluff that towers close against the water. Up-stream of the bluff a large maple leans well out over the water from the left bank. The bluff face is partially ob-scured in summer, but as you come around the curve, it becomes obvious just how pretty it is. You can see the iron-stained rock low on the face shining through the trees much more clearly as you draw abreast of it. There is a vertical cave mouth low on the cliff in the middle of the largest red section. There are other cave entrances lower down, but only one of them is easily accessible.

High up on the overhang above the caves is a group of twisted cedars that may have been looking down over the scene for over a thousand years. Some of the cedars on Ozark streams have been shown to be among the oldest trees in the world.

After passing this bluff the creek returns to its straight, gently curving character through shallows and bars that are more and more overgrown as the summer wears on. When you come to a low bluff bordering the stream on the right, watch for the small cave twenty feet above water level and about halfway down its face.

After a little break in the bluff where a couple of gullies

slice through, a rounded bulge of rock protrudes out into the water above a cabin-sized boulder that stands well away from the cliff face. This big rock has several trees growing on its crown, and their roots are beginning the process of splitting the boulder from top to bottom. The stream swerves around this spot in a beautiful, curving pool where a small road touches the bank on the left.

After some shallow runs, the bluff on the left tapers down along a vertical rock face to a height of about ten feet at a series of shallow ledges immediately above the water. Around the next bend is a forty-foot cliff of sheer rock that begins downstream of a very big hole where the creek swings back to the left. At the upstream end of this pool, over the deepest water, a huge cave mouth lies partially hidden behind some obscuring trees. During the first spring that I fished Big Creek, I passed right by this cave without seeing it, and I was startled on a trip that same fall at how easily it is seen when the leaves have dropped.

The cave proper doesn't go back very far into the rock, but there is a big room inside the cave mouth that is an excellent shelter. Someone has built a sturdy table and left it standing in the main room for use on camping trips. Look carefully for the cave if the foliage is thick. There is deep, fish-filled water for seventy-five yards below its mouth.

Past the next curve to the right is an undercut bluff on the left with caves extending beneath it at water level. Look for the piles of peeled limbs inside the low caves that indicate some clever beavers have been using them for a home. There is a deep pool at the end of the bluff as the creek bears slightly to the right.

As I was hiking in this spot to prepare for this chapter, a rock lodged under the tongue of my right shoe, directly over my instep. The pressure soon got so bothersome that I had to remove the offending stone. As I sat on a convenient log and loosened the laces on my shoe, I thought of numerous times on earlier hikes when I had stubbornly walked too far with pebbles in irritating spots, not wanting to be bothered with a stop to take them out. I suppose I thought that they would eventually work themselves around to a more comfortable position, but that seldom happened. Thinking like that only led to painful injuries that hobbled me for the remainder of the hike. I have learned over the years that a little time taken in cleaning out your shoes at the first indication of discomfort can save considerable time and pain later. It's a good idea to stop about once an hour to dump out any accumulated rocks, even if they haven't become a great nuisance.

There is no more deep water through the point at which a nice spring branch flows in from the left. A faint road strikes the creek nearby on that same side. It goes back along the little tributary and soon skirts the edge of a large beaver pond. This pond and its dam are usually well maintained, and at times the spot is a good place to fish. From the pond the road climbs the ridge and angles back down to the stream below the iron-stained bluff you encountered upstream.

On the other side of Big Creek, opposite the spring branch, a ridge stands well back from the bank, high among thick trees that obscure it almost totally in summer. It is an interesting area to walk along in fall and winter, but the tangled undergrowth makes it a spot to avoid in warmer seasons.

Downstream of a slough that runs back toward the distant ridge, a well-traveled road crosses diagonally down to the right after you pass a pool full of lily pads. Follow the road to the right, keeping to the forks that turn toward the water. You will soon come to an open camping area where another road enters from up the ridge. This clearing borders a long pool beneath another impressive bluff on the far side.

The road continues through thick trees and comes out at a wide section of the creek along beautiful, curving riffles. Slightly upstream of the road's emergence on a high dirt bank, there is another very large cave opening that can be hard to see from a distance. This cave is another that has only one big room, but it is one that you

should see because of the many jumbled rock masses that
have fallen from the roof all over its floor. If you are here
in early spring, you will find the beauty of the slope
below the cave is magnified by the blossoms of several
lovely redbud trees. This whole valley is filled with an
unusual number of flowering trees in spring.

Return to the road and you will find it runs parallel to
the stream, past a circular turnaround, and down to the
water, where it crosses to a high dirt bank at a downstream slant. You can follow this road for nearly a mile,
through woods, overgrown fields, and finally across open
pastures, before coming to another ford. This crossing is
at a right-angle bend along the highest cliff on Big Creek.

To make certain you see two exceptional caves, I would
suggest a walk along the creek here on your downstream
hike. Take the road when you hike back up if you need to
save some time.

To reach the caves, bear to the right along a high-water
channel past the next big hole downstream of the road
crossing and walk along the base of the ridge. Look carefully about twenty feet above you for the first cave. Its
low slit of an opening will make you stoop to enter, but
the ceiling rises quickly once you get inside, where you
can stand comfortably in a circular room. At first glance
the cave seems to end just behind a very low crawl space
at the rear, but if you have a flashlight you will find that
the floor drops away beyond this low-ceilinged spot into
a very large room.

The floor is very uneven, with big depressions that are
filled with water in rainy seasons, and the passage goes
back well over a hundred feet into the hillside. Near the
front of this second room is a large crack in the floor that
in the past was easily wide enough for me to climb down
into. Since then a large chunk of the ceiling has fallen
into this crevice and blocked it almost completely.
A small person might still be able to squeeze past this
blockage and go deeper into the cave, but don't try it if
you are alone. When the water is up, this lower portion is
flooded.

The second level of this cave could be interesting for experienced spelunkers to explore, but I have never gone more than a few yards beyond the crack in the floor, and have no idea what a more adventuresome person might find there. It was a pleasant surprise for me when I discovered the size and beauty of the parts of the cave I did go into. There are some unusual formations on the ceiling in several spots, and the cave is home to a small colony of bats.

A little past this cave you will find another, this one with a mouth tall enough to contain a two-story house. It lies about the same distance above you on the slope as the first cave and opens twenty yards before you get to the large split boulder that sits against the base of the hill. The cave is essentially a single large room that gradually slopes upward. It narrows for over a hundred feet until ending in a small chamber.

I once sat out a severe thunderstorm inside this cave mouth early in the spring. It is a comfortable, secure haven with a lovely view of the stream when the trees are still bare of leaves, as they were that day. One of the many nice things about upper Big Creek is that there are so many caves you can take shelter in if the weather is threatening.

After some shallow rapids downstream, the creek gradually deepens into a long run that contains the greatest number of consecutive deep-water pools anywhere on Big Creek. You can catch fish at virtually any point for the next five hundred yards. When the water is up even a little, you will have to get out on the bank and walk around some of the deeper sections. It does not get shallow again until the big turn along the high bluff ahead of you.

Watch for no-trespassing signs on the fences along the fields by this pool. On some of my hikes I have seen such signs on the fences here. At other times I have seen those signs on the ground and some nonsensical ones put up in their place. Obviously there has been a continuing problem here, and I would be especially careful to avoid fenced property. Don't become part of a problem caused by some other person.

At the ford past the lower end of the deep water, you can cross to the gravel bar on the right and follow ATV tracks downstream. Look across the creek atop the high cliff in front of you for a deer stand that must have the best view of any in the country. I really wonder if someone actually shoots deer along the stream from that elevation. I suppose it's possible, but I shudder to think how long it would take to get down to the deer after it had been shot—particularly an animal that is only wounded. That thought is especially disturbing to me.

After you cross the ford and follow the tracks through the wooded bar, they cross the creek again and parallel the water through an overgrown field. The tracks end at a fence on the edge of the woods.

I usually stay in the creek at the second ford and fish downstream through a portion that has occasional deep water for the next half mile. At the large, dry creek channel that enters from the right, you have come about four miles on your hike.

In another quarter of a mile, more ATV tracks cross the creek before you reach a gently sloping ridge that has deep water among jumbled rocks at its base. There is then nothing much of interest until you get to the ridge you have been walking toward for half a mile, where a large pool of deep water bends to the left along the base of the ridge. A cliff with a vertical slit of a cave opening in its face is visible around the next turn.

Farther down the cliff what seems from a distance to be merely a large overhang of rock is actually a beautiful cave with a gaping mouth. The cave entrance is bordered by a wide ledge, stretching like a comfortable patio along the creek. The back of the ledge slopes gently upward from barely two feet above normal water level and would make an ideal camping sight for the overnight hiker or fisherman. There isn't much evidence that people have camped at the cave, probably because the creek here is too deep to wade across except in very dry seasons, and steep rock faces make the spot hard to reach from both upstream and downstream.

The cave is eye-catching, especially at its entrance, but it doesn't go back more than seventy-five or eighty feet. Another, smaller cave mouth a short distance past this big one seems to go back well into the rock, but I have not explored it because it is so low I would have to crawl to get inside.

Less than a hundred yards downstream of these caves, on the same side of the creek, is a slender, isolated column of rock about thirty feet high that can legitimately be called a pedestal formation or rock chimney. It stands directly against the stream bank hundreds of feet away from any other rock outcroppings. When viewed from diagonally downstream, the formation has an unusual button-nosed human profile that I first noticed when looking at my photos of the spot.

Immediately below the pedestal rock is a fine pool over a hundred yards long. A road comes in from the right before you reach the next long stretch of deep water a bit farther downstream. The road runs parallel to the creek around the stretch of deep water and makes a convenient path for the hiker to follow.

I was once scared within an inch of my life on this little section of road when I walked right into the middle of a flock of wild turkeys. Before I even suspected their presence, they were taking off directly in front of me and flying into everything that wouldn't get out of their way. When I finally realized what was happening and my heart started beating again, the only trace of them was a few feathers drifting down from some shaking limbs— four of them mine.

There are a few woodcocks in some of the damp, shaded woods along the creek, and sometimes they are even harder on my nerves than those wild turkeys. Woodcocks will often wait until an intruder is practically on top of them before they launch themselves from the ground. Far too often they flutter up from my feet and dart back and forth through the trees with total disregard for my blood pressure.

At times the flow of the stream here may go underground, but it reappears in a few yards. Other lovely pools and bluffs line the high ridges ahead; they are certainly worth seeing if you have time to continue the hike. You are about a half mile from the two big pools that mark the end of the flowing portion of the upper stream in the drier seasons. From the lower of the two pools, Big Creek flows underground for six to eight miles in times of drought. Watch the time and judge the distance you have yet to hike. You will not have time to get to the last of the deep holes and the large cave above it unless you start out very early in the morning.

Those familiar with the logging roads which crisscross these hills probably know of several spots along this portion of the creek that could be used as endpoints for this hike, but I haven't tried any of them. My recommendation is that you stop your hike here and retrace your steps to the parking spot at Bear Claw Spring.

7

BIG CREEK ━━━━━━━━━━━━━

County Road 3710 to the Current River
(Map 4, p. 46)

There are at least three different ways to hike the lower portions of Big Creek, all with their own starting points. The first originates where the hike up the middle section of the creek begins, past the end of KK Highway north of Hartshorn at the low-water bridge on County Road 3710. Park in the area to the left of the road before the stream crossing and walk downstream from that point.

This hike in the summer traverses five miles of dry gravel beds before you come to any appreciable water in the creek, and two more miles of walking before you get to the Current River. If you have taken the hike upstream from the low-water bridge, you have probably seen enough dry creek beds to last you for a while. I have not repeated the downstream hike from here for many years, preferring the other two ways of reaching the mouth of Big Creek. However, if you do wish to walk this entire section, I would recommend doing so in the fall after the leaves have dropped, so any rock outcroppings and caves that may be hidden behind the vegetation are more easily seen.

A second, much shorter hike entails continuing on K Highway beyond its intersection with KK, going about four miles past the Shannon County line to County Road 385.

Follow this small gravel road north until it angles down toward the creek. There it passes between two farms and parallels the creek for a short distance behind the out-buildings of one of the farms. Don't despair of finding the creek as you drive down 385. The road is about ten miles long, but it is neither unduly rough nor steep until the short slope down to the creek. There are two parking places on the creek side of the road before it passes through a cattle gap and crosses the stream at a gravel ford. If you have a four-wheel-drive vehicle you can continue on this road. Bear right at the first intersection and you will come out on the Current River at a spot called Cedar Grove, immediately above the mouth of Big Creek.

The hike from the ford on 385 to the river is only about two miles. The stream is flowing throughout, but the scenery and water depth are less than impressive until you near the Current River. This is another hike I do not often take, much preferring the third possibility, but you may want to plot all three hikes on a contour map before deciding which best suits you.

The third hike also involves driving down 385 for most of its length. A hundred yards before you come to the hill that slopes down to the creek valley, turn right on County Road 394. This little road is about four miles long and in places is much narrower and steeper than 385, but until you come out of the woods into the fields bordering the Current River, there are no spots where you should be in danger of getting stuck. Once the road heads back to the left past the woods, however, there are several bad mud-holes in wet weather. They are a danger, due to their deep ruts, even when they are dry. Be careful in these spots. Pull over and park if you are in the least doubtful about making it through. This area is quite remote and not a place to risk getting stuck.

All the little tracks turning off downhill to the right lead toward the river. You can explore along one of them if you would rather have more of your hike run upstream along the Current River. I usually park along the fields short of a wide bed of deep mud and soft sand that extends completely across any possible pathway through a little ravine. This spot stands in water year-round. The road ahead branches several times; walk down the most-traveled portion, bearing left when it divides. The correct road roughly follows the electric lines that run across the field and down the slope to the north. As you enter the last patch of woods before the river, there is a small, old building on the right that has a concrete foundation and looks as though it could have been a one-room school. Don't try to step inside, as the floors are getting dangerously weak.

A few yards away the road reaches the Current River and crosses a shallow riffle to the other side. Close upstream on the left is Medlock Cave, which you should make the effort to find and explore. The cave is impressive and has an underground lake in its depths. On the opposite bank, less than a mile downstream, you will find Welch Spring, at the site of an old sanitarium. The spring is the sixth largest in the state and was once used for rearing rainbow trout. The large cave at the spring has been explored via canoes. With a little careful navigating, it is not too hard to cross the river by Welch Spring and find your way back to your car across the fields on the west bank.

Separated by beautiful runs and rapids, many deep holes lie in the river above the crossing by Medlock Cave. As you hike up to Big Creek you will find that the Current River is crowded with canoes full of tourists in the warmer months. If you are interested in fishing, don't let the canoes worry you. The fish seem to get used to them, and I have caught smallmouth bass and trout within seconds of the passage of a group of floaters. The trout in this section of the river are escapees from the put-and-take trout-fishing area at Montauk State Park about ten miles up the river. Some of these trout can be real lunkers. The biggest I have caught weighed about two pounds, but I have seen much larger fish swirling away from me in the clear, cold waters.

The road runs up the right side of the river in heavy woods and crosses back to the left through fields and patches of trees as it cuts off a big curve. At another ford it returns to the east bank and leads across large fields until it bends back to the left for a short distance through the woods, coming out on the river opposite the mouth of Big Creek at Cedar Grove.

There is usually a well-tended beaver dam in the lower reaches of Big Creek in a straight wooded section that is normally quite shallow. Above a bend to the right, you will come to some thirty- to forty-foot bluffs that are dotted with small caves. A second bluff a few yards upstream is not at all high, but the creek is so small and the valley so narrow that your closeness to its pitted red-and-black-stained surface makes it an outstanding sight.

From here on up to the 385 ford the creek swings through wide, sweeping curves among two-hundred-foot ridges. The valley gets progressively wider and the gravel bars more pronounced. A short distance past 385, the flow runs intermittently underground. For a one-way hike you could leave one vehicle near the ford and take another down along the Current River as just described.

In my travels I have learned that there is an even easier way to get to the mouth of Big Creek and Cedar Grove. At the intersection of the creek and County Road 3710 north of Hartshorn, follow the road across the low-water bridge over Big Creek and up the ridges on the far side. When you intersect a hard-surfaced road, you have reached B Highway east of Raymondville. Follow it to the right until the pavement ends and take the gravel road to the right at the T intersection. In half a mile you will reach the Current River at the mouth of Big Creek. Follow the road to the left and it will take you to the low-water bridge over the Current River at Cedar Grove.

Without having to do any walking to reach this point, you have a wide range of choices for hiking. It is great fun to go up and down the river fishing for the large rainbow trout that hide in its cold, swift rapids and dark, shaded pools. You can also walk as far back up Big Creek as your time and energy permit, but note that the scenery on this part of the creek is not that impressive and the water supply is usually scanty.

MAP 5

Ashley Creek

(Chapter 8)

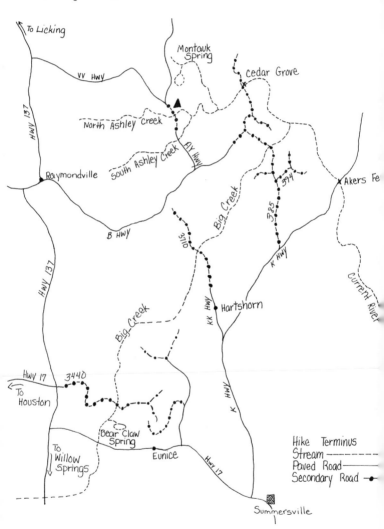

8

ASHLEY CREEK ═══════════════

(Map 5)

Ashley Creek is a short stream that flows into the Current River a few miles below the trout-fishing area at Montauk State Park. The scenery varies from shady and intimate in secluded sections to wide, sweeping vistas across huge oxbows that run through gently rolling pastures. The hike down to the Current River is only about three miles, and the smallmouth fishing can be excellent.

One August afternoon I caught sixteen smallmouth of keeping size in Ashley Creek within a two-hour period, returning all of them to the water. It is especially important to practice catch-and-release fishing in such tiny waterways, or they will soon be fished out. Once you get to the Current River, you are also in great trout water. Rainbow trout are commonly taken for several miles in both directions from the mouth of Ashley Creek.

To reach Ashley Creek, take Highway 137 to B Highway at Raymondville by either driving north from Willow Springs for thirty miles or going twelve miles south from Licking. Follow B Highway to its intersection with AY and continue down AY to its end, turning right when the pavement gives way to gravel. If you stay on B Highway to its end and turn right on the gravel road at the T intersection, you will come to the mouth of Big Creek on the

Current River. The area below the bridge over the Current River at Cedar Grove is described in the previous chapter.

The first creek crossing the road past the end of AY is South Ashley Creek. It has only a tiny flow after extended periods of dry weather. There are no parking spots along the road here. At the next crossing, which is North Ashley Creek, there is parking on the left of the road before you get to the low-water bridge. The creek is quite small for the first half mile or so downstream. It gets noticeably larger after North and South Ashley creeks join at the end of the first big bend to the right. There is a small bit of deep water back up the south branch a few yards short of its mouth. The left bank of North Ashley Creek is posted below the bridge where your hike begins. There are houses all along that side. As always, respect private property and obey no-trespassing signs.

After South Ashley Creek enters the main stream, there is a bend to the left with some deep water littered with fallen trees. Around this bend you will come to a small bluff on the right that has a little cave about ten feet above water level at its upper end. The cave is hard to see because of screening trees, and you must look carefully to keep from missing it. A dirt road leads across the field to the left toward houses and barns.

This field continues for a half mile along the north bank, while a wooded ridge borders the creek on the south. At a ten-foot bluff along this ridge, there is a pleasant fishing hole that usually holds from one to three nice smallmouth. All the spots that are even moderately deep along the creek commonly have good fish populations.

A road crosses the creek before it bends sharply to the right along the foot of the high ridge you have been approaching. It leads toward the barns visible to the left and another barn that is out of sight nearly a mile to the south. Fish the pools above the little road carefully. Some of the largest fish in the creek hide among the logs here, but they are easy to spook.

Ashley Creek runs straight to the right along the heavily wooded ridge beyond the road crossing. There are stretches of shallow and deep water alternating throughout the length of this long run, continuing well past the point the hillside tapers down into open pastures. I once caught a twelve-inch smallmouth along this ridge, using a technique that is a little out of the ordinary. Casting over the end of a sycamore limb ten feet above the water, I reeled my plastic worm to the surface to keep the hooks from tangling in the tree and waded up to take the lure off my line before pulling the line through the branches. As my bait splashed, half in and half out of the water, the smallmouth grabbed it and started leaping all over the pool, fighting to break free. I stood there with my mouth open and watched the antics of the fish. When he was finally exhausted and I was over my amazement, I reeled him up to the limb, which was pulled down almost to water level by his weight, and freed my line from the tree. After releasing the smallmouth, I congratulated myself for the clever method I had just developed for presenting a lure without letting my line frighten the fish.

Near the end of the wooded section of this long, straight run, a fence crosses the creek, and a little farther downstream a small spring branch comes in from the left. Below here Ashley Creek sweeps to the left in a huge horseshoe bend that cuts through extensive open fields. A big barn is visible far up the slope to the right, and there is another barn on the inside of the peninsula formed by the meandering of the creek. The mound off to the left, which resembles a dam paralleling the bank of the stream, is actually a natural levee. It marks the point where floodwaters stop and drop their load of debris, building the levee higher and higher with the passing years. Take some time to fish the pockets of deep water that have been scoured out at intervals all along the outside of this lengthy curve.

The downstream end of the big horseshoe bend switches back in a smaller but equally sharp turn to the right with much deep water and numerous projecting ledges all along its length. The creek straightens out past low-lying rocks that border a deep pool on the left after the field on the right ends. Back in the trees farther downstream is a tall ridge with a shaded bluff on its lower face that has a small round cave mouth about fifteen feet up its rock front. This cave is hard to get to because of the steepness of the slope and the depth of the pool beneath it. Below the cave at water level is a low ledge with an opening underneath that could be another cave. It is hard to judge how far it goes back under the water. The bluff grows higher, with even deeper pools bordering it, before the creek bends to the left and splashes along swiftly to the Current River.

The river is shallow and easily waded in this region. It is obvious when you wade from the creek into the river how much colder the water becomes. You are only about three miles below Montauk State Park, where the majority of the flow of the river originates. Rainbow trout can be taken from these icy waters using crayfish, minnows, or a variety of jigs or streamers. Try your own favorite lures if you are experienced in fishing for trout. The rainbow in the river are escapees from the fee area at Montauk, and some have grown to lunker size in the fertile, icy waters. Take your time to fish both upstream and downstream from the mouth of Ashley Creek before starting your trip back up to your car.

MAP 6

Leatherwood Creek

(Chapter 9)

9

LEATHERWOOD CREEK ═══════

(Map 6)

Leatherwood Creek is a memorable six miles of beaver ponds lining a narrow canyon of a valley that is drained by a tiny spring-fed creek on its way down from one of the most impressive geologic wonders of Missouri. This creek is one of my favorite places to hike in the entire Ozarks. Its towering bluffs, rock columns, and crystalline waters draw you upstream toward the massive, ancient curve of Leatherwood Arch, one of the two largest such spans in Missouri. The arch is flanked by two caves: an unusual curving tunnel on the opposite side a short distance downstream, and the very deep, wide-mouthed Leatherwood Cave a hundred yards upstream, high up on the steep bluff to the north.

The depths of Big Cave, with its lovely, splashing waterfall, and the narrow opening of Peter Renfro Cave await the hiker about a mile farther upstream. The prospect of seeing the four caves and the arch would be reason enough for an outing on Leatherwood Creek, but they turn out to be only incidental attractions for this outing. The beauty that awaits at every turn of the creek, along every bluff, in every beaver pond, makes each day spent on Leatherwood Creek one of the most satisfying times you will ever spend in the outdoors.

The jumping-off point for this hike lies down Highway 106 east of Summersville. Drive past D Highway and the Flat Rock lookout tower to the turnoff on Shannon County Road 106–425, a half mile past the high-voltage power lines that pass over Highway 106. Turn south down 425 for a delightful, twisting drive down to the Jacks Fork valley. The road is sheltered by thick stands of trees and is kept in excellent condition.

As 425 levels off at the valley floor, you will see an Ozark Scenic Riverways sign on the left beyond a little dry wash—you are nearing the river. Another sign warns that the area is subject to flash flooding, so be alert if thunderstorms threaten.

Soon you will enter a beautiful campground along Jacks Fork at the mouth of Bay Creek. This comfortable area is complete with picnic tables, rest rooms, trash barrels, and hitching posts for your horse. Bay Creek is narrow and short, but it flows here even in the driest seasons. A trip up the steep, rugged valley of this creek makes an interesting little hike of its own. It enters Jacks Fork to the left of the point where 425 crosses the creek at a gravel ford. The road continues up the north bank of the river toward Leatherwood Creek, about two miles upstream.

Park in the campground and cross the ford on foot, unless you have a four-wheel-drive vehicle. It would be easy to get stuck in the loose gravel in an ordinary car. The road runs up the river beneath high bluffs that are worth the effort of walking down to the river and looking high above you to see them from a better angle. There are good camping spots along this well-tended lane at several Park Service campgrounds.

Where the road turns sharply to the right between two rest rooms, a narrow trail goes straight ahead to the river. Take the turn up the hill. When you have crossed the open field to the north, take the branch of the road that leads westward through the trees along the base of the ridge ahead. This ridge has another impressive bluff on its upper slopes, but it is impossible to see from so close at hand.

The last time I took this hike was in late September, and the early brightening colors of sumac, columbine, sassafras, dogwood, black gum, spice bushes, hickory, and sycamore were already splashing through the fading green of the woods. The brightest color of all was captured in the flashy red leaves of the poison ivy. Their beauty belied the danger of the painful rash they could still cause on that crisp day in early fall.

Bright red berries decorated dogwood, spice bushes, and sassafras with gaudy little ornaments, and the sassafras reminded me of the pleasant uses I have made of the plant in the past. Most people know that you can boil the roots of sassafras to make a fragrant, root-beer-flavored tea, but few have ever made use of the berries. Roast the berries in a slow oven until they are a medium brown color, grind them into a powder, and then use them in the same way that you would use cocoa. It is an amazingly good substitute. The dried and powdered leaves of sassafras make the thickening substance called file (pronounced *fee-lay*) that is often used in Cajun cooking.

Sassafras trees are easily identified. Their smooth-margined leaves come in three distinctive shapes. One is smoothly elliptical; another has a small lobe on one side that makes it look like a mitten; a third has thumblike lobes on both sides. Of course, the root-beer scent of the freshly dug roots is the sure clue.

This section of the road ends at the river with parking spots on the high bank on the right. Going past the parking area, cross over to the left side of the stream. A vertical cliff drops off into the deep water across the river ahead of you. Where the cliff falls away, wade back across to the right and find the road running up the downstream side of the little spring branch that comes into the river here. The branch drains along the lower edge of a broad tributary valley that has the mouth of Leatherwood Creek on its far side. This creek drains from a lovely marshy spot about a half mile to the north that is a treasure of wildflowers in the spring and summer.

Follow the dirt road across the spring flow and hike

back into the edge of the woods across the wide field to the north. A few yards into the woods you will come to the first crossing of Leatherwood Creek, a half mile above its mouth. The lower portion of the creek is pretty, but this hike is long, and it has to be a round-trip, so keep to the road and go on upstream. The really beautiful spots are ahead of you.

When you reach the creek, you will notice that its water is much colder than that in Jacks Fork because of the many small springs upstream. Leatherwood Creek is tiny, but its flow is steady, even in a dry fall. Some of the streams in this book become faint reflections of their springtime flows late in the year, and the fishing in them dwindles to practically nothing, but Leatherwood has a dozen or more marvelous beaver ponds along its course, making it as pretty in September as it is in May. Without the beaver dams there would be little deep water anywhere in the valley.

The ATV road you are following is also used by many on horseback who take advantage of this convenient path into an area of terrific scenery. The road travels along the stream almost all the way to the upper end of this hike, crossing back and forth time after time as the channel switches from one side of the valley to the other.

The narrow track crosses the creek the first time between two deep pools and leads upstream to ford the stream fourteen more times before turning away up a tributary valley and going up along the ridges. Stay to the right along the creek at the first two intersections beyond the first ford, where side roads lead away to the west. Steep bluffs parallel the creek on either side for the next four miles, with sheer cliffs, overhanging ledges, and columnlike rock formations throughout.

After the third crossing, the road runs along a sort of swampy slough before coming out at an attractive open area of the creek that has a beautiful rock face high above. This valley is exceptionally narrow and the sides are unusually high to be bordering such a small stream. The bluff curves gently away to the left ahead of you. A short distance upstream, when you are on the right bank, high cliffs with a few small cave openings extend far above, partly obscured by thick trees. I usually walk over to the creek at intervals to fish and look at the scenery.

Leatherwood Creek is named for a small tree that grows commonly along its banks. The bark and small branches of the leatherwood tree are as strong and supple as leather, and early settlers used them as emergency replacements for broken leather straps—hence the name. The Indians who inhabited the area used strips of leatherwood bark as fishing lines, bindings for spear and arrow points, and the like.

After you have returned to the left side of the creek, another sheer rock face is visible to the right, and there is an attractive overhang a little above the crossing. The road leads well away from the creek through what seems to be a permanent little pool, perhaps from a spring, that is alive with minnows and small fish. Take some time to quietly fish the many beaver ponds you will pass by as the road winds its way up the stream. The ponds are all deep enough to hold good fish, but the waters are so clear that you must be very careful not to spook them back into the shadows.

Beyond the tenth ford a road comes down the hill from the right. Keep going straight ahead. I was nearly run over by two hunters on four-wheelers right here in early September. They came roaring down the hill and slid around the intersection so fast that they almost bumped into me as I tried to get off the creek side of the road. If you hear any vehicles coming, get well off into the bushes; some riders are not as careful and polite as they should be.

The next time you cross over to the left bank, follow the spring branch that enters the creek at the downstream side of the ford. It pours from the ground at a wide seepage area that lies to the side of a clearing at the top of the slope. There is no actual pool here. Some rocks have been piled up in a small cairn near a cedar tree alongside the road to mark the spot. The spring is very cold, and in great part accounts for the icy temperature of the water in the creek below it.

I have caught a kind of fish from the beaver ponds on the upper creek that I have only come across in a few of the small streams I have fished in the Ozarks. The first time I noticed the slender pikelike fish hanging suspended in the shaded waters of Leatherwood Creek, I thought I must be seeing things. But after a few casts I had one of the madly jumping little fighters in the shallow water at the edge of the pool and could see that it was indeed a grass pickerel. Carefully removing the hook with long-nosed pliers to save my fingers from the sharp, wicked teeth, I released it.

Grass pickerel grow to be no more than sixteen to eighteen inches in length, but they are voracious hunters. In a pool far upstream, I once saw a pickerel that seemed to have an unusual, misshapen head. Feeling a little sorry for it, I slipped along the bank to get a closer look. When I could see it more clearly, I laughed to discover that the miniature glutton had caught and almost swallowed a longear sunfish that was a good deal bigger than the pickerel's own mouth. I have heard people accused of having eyes that were bigger than their stomachs, but this hungry character was ridiculous. The sunfish was about two-thirds swallowed, through jaws that were distended around it in a most uncomfortable-looking manner. I suppose that oversized meal gradually worked its way down and the pickerel eventually finished its long, drawn-out digestion, but it really made an unusual sight on that pretty September day.

When you wade the last ford and the road veers away to the left up a steep valley, the creek widens into the most spectacular beaver pond on its entire length. Stay along the stream above here. Wade up the narrow runs, which grow progressively smaller, and skirt the edges of the beaver ponds that still dot the creek. There are no roads along this part of Leatherwood Creek. It flows through a steep, canyonlike section of the valley that is narrower than at any point downstream, and there is very little room along the banks for a road.

When you see the rather well worn track of an ATV road crossing the creek, there are high bluffs on both sides, with a cliff on the right that is extremely steep and beautiful. Keep your eyes trained on its upper face. About a hundred yards before the right-angle bend of the creek to the left, one of the largest, most beautiful natural arches in the entire state towers far above you: Leatherwood Arch never fails to impress.

Books that I have read compare its size to that of the Hootentown Arch on the James River. They may be about the same size, but the Leatherwood Arch is much closer and easier to see, thereby giving the sense of being much bigger. The bluff here is so steep that you cannot climb to the arch from directly below. If you want to reach the top, go back downstream and come up the gentler slope.

A few yards before the sharp bend upstream, the wide, flat mouth of a deep cave opens thirty feet up the north bank of the creek. Leatherwood Cave has an oddly shaped, almost rectangular opening that looks somewhat artificial, but it is a natural cave, complete with stalactites, stalagmites, and columns. Some of the formations are still growing, as you can tell from the sheen of the mineral-laden water slipping slowly down their sides. You can go back several hundred feet into the ridge before the cave roof lowers enough to force you to crawl.

On the south wall of the valley, a little downstream from the arch, a smaller cave opens at the end of a projecting prominence. It is actually a forty-foot tunnel that has openings on the north and west faces of this corner of the bluff. One September I found the remains of a turkey in the cave. From the tracks and scratches on the rocks, it looked as if a bobcat had done the bird in and feasted long and well in this rocky shelter. One mile beyond the sharp bend upstream, past another series of large beaver ponds, the two branches of Leatherwood Creek come together to form the stream you are following. Stay to the left at this junction and in a few hundred yards you will come to the picture-postcard beauty of Big Cave, which opens invitingly at water level on the north bank of the stream. Through a separate little tunnel on the upstream side of the cave mouth, an attractive waterfall splashes down about four feet into the creek. The cave goes far back into the cliff, and an opening in the ceiling beyond the first bend to the left gives promise of deeper tunnels beyond. Once you have found Big Cave, you should go back downstream to the first steep valley that slants in from the south and walk up to the ledge over which the intermittent stream sometimes drops in a wet-weather fall. Look on the western side of this ledge for the slit entrance to Peter Renfro Cave. The opening is very low and unimpressive, but the cave quickly opens into a roomy chamber that goes back over one hundred feet into the hillside.

There is virtually no more deep water and little interesting scenery above this point on the creek. I always end my hikes here. The only reasonable way back to your starting point is to walk down the stream until you reach the road you followed upstream, returning to your car along the same path you used earlier. If you want to include more of Jacks Fork in your return trip, cut back to your right after the last ford and follow Leatherwood Creek to its mouth. There are several good holes along this part of the river that can yield good fish on occasion.

MAP 7

North Prong of Jacks Fork

(Chapter 10)

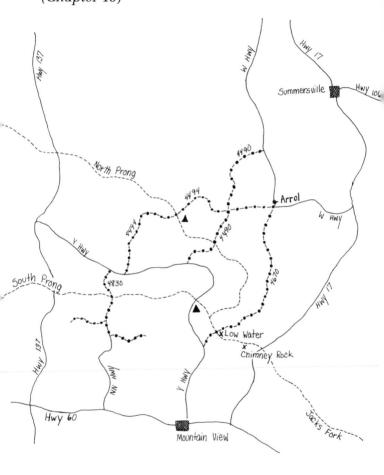

Hwy 137

W HWY

Hwy 17

Summersville

Hwy 106

North Prong

4490

4494

Arrol

W HWY

Y HWY

4494

4490

4670

Hwy 17

South Prong

4830

Hwy 137

X Low Water

X Chimney Rock

NN HWY

Y HWY

Hwy 60

Jacks Fork

Mountain View

Hike Terminus   ▲
Stream - - - - - - - -
Paved Road —————
Secondary Road •—•—•—•

10

NORTH PRONG OF JACKS FORK ════════════

Kinard Ranch to Chimney Rock
(Map 7)

       A pleasant hike on the North Prong begins below a low concrete dam at Kinard Ranch, two miles off Y Highway north of Mountain View. Drive past the new bridge over the South Prong on Y Highway to Texas County Road 4494 at the small wooden sign to Kinard Ranch. The intersection of 4830, leading over to the upper South Prong, is only two hundred yards farther up on the left. Turn east on 4494 and proceed to the low-water bridge over the North Prong. It runs below a six-foot-high dam that impounds a beautiful pool extending several hundred yards up the river. There are several parking spots on the far side of the bridge.

    Another vehicle can be left downstream at the spot called Low Water to make this a one-way hike. Park in the area used at the end of the hike down the South Prong. It lies below the Y Highway bridge, six miles north of Mountain View. You can turn east on County Road 4670, the gravel road south of the bridge, and park on the far side of the low-water bridge at the confluence of the North and South Prongs of Jacks Fork. There are several places to park along the field extending upstream beside the North Prong. These would be more convenient for the end of the hike, but the dirt tracks through this field can be very slippery in wet weather. If things are a little muddy, go back to the spot at the highway bridge.

Below the bridge at the upper end of the hike, the river plunges over a succession of rock ledges. These splashing cascades drop into a beautiful pool that is a popular swimming hole for people who live in the area. Look for the rope hanging from the tree on the west bank. It makes a great spot to swing out into the cold water on a hot summer day.

An attractive spring rises along the left bank above the ledges and tumbles down to the creek through the boulders on that side. A short distance past this spring, two smaller flows rise and contribute their waters to the river. Beavers try to dam up these spring channels with regularity, but floods wreck every attempt.

Fields line the river on both sides as you begin your hike, but there are many dead trees along the banks and thick oak forests covering the nearby ridges. This combination of standing dead trees and living timber makes the area a perfect home for its thriving colony of red-headed woodpeckers. These beautiful birds have completely red heads without a crest. Their heads and the large white areas on their wings distinguish these medium-sized woodpeckers from their many cousins. I can't begin to describe their raucous call, but once you hear it, you will never mistake them for any other bird. They are uncommon locally; the only nearby spot where I have seen so many lies along the overflow from Alley Spring down to Jacks Fork west of Eminence.

The first real bend in the river is a sharp one to the left along a fifteen-foot bluff bordering the open field to the south. There are extensive flat sheets of limestone patterned with wave or ripple marks along the outside of this curve, and a moderate hole of deep water begins as the river eases back toward the ridge ahead.

A road now crosses from the field on the right and leads over toward the buildings that stand beside the county road along which you parked. At a big swing to

The tunnel opening and pool on the downstream side of "The Sinks" on Sinking Creek.

Unique bluff along Sinking Creek near Highway 19, a short distance above Camp Zoe.

A large spring against an over-grown bluff near Big Creek below Mauser Mill.

Icicles decorate a small ledge above Big Creek near Mauser Mill.

Mill Mountain Shut-in and Klepzig Mill on lower Rocky Creek.

The upper section of Buzzard Mountain Shut-in on Rocky Creek.

Flowering dogwood in Prairie Hollow Canyon.

An unusual pine with a trunk twisted into a complete horizontal circle. Near Big Creek west of Hartshorn.

Iron-and-manganese-stained bluff along Big Creek below Bear Claw Spring.

Stone "head" atop a pedestal formation on Big Creek below Bear Claw Spring.

The shaded face of a bluff on the lower reaches of Ashley Creek near the Current River.

Big Cave near the headwaters of Leatherwood Creek. The small cave with the waterfall is entirely separate from the larger opening for several yards into the cliff.

A well-tended beaver dam on lower Leatherwood Creek imme-diately above one of the many fords.

Fall foliage along the North Prong of Jacks Fork south of County Road 4490.

Chimney Rock on Jacks Fork below the junction of the North and South Prongs at Low Water.

the south along the next ridge, there is a spring branch flowing in at the very beginning of the curve. It drops over uneven ledges a few yards back up its course in an enclosed gully that must be even more attractive when the flow over the falls is magnified after a rain.

The ridge becomes steeper as the stream meanders along its base and scattered pockets of deep water interrupt the swift, shallow flows. Watch the rock outcroppings along the ridge for occasional entrances to small caves. The ridge pulls back from the river for a while until it angles back in at a rock prominence that stands about sixty feet over the water. The stream is deflected around this handsome outcrop into a deep pool below its downstream end. It then runs out toward the middle of the valley through large gravel bars on both sides. The road that runs along the right bank leads to the house and outbuildings of a farm. Stay on the gravel bars to the left. The average depth of the water in the river this far upstream is surprising even in the dry seasons of the year. Deep holes dot the streambed with regularity as the channel angles back to the left and wanders through the open valley ahead.

Most of the bass are small in this part of the river, but there are usually plenty of them. I caught a pair of acrobatic fish from each of three consecutive holes in this section of the stream during October while I was preparing this chapter. A couple were over fourteen inches, and they reminded me emphatically that smallmouth jump and fight even more than usual when the first crisp days of fall add their stimulating chill to the waters.

At the next ridge the North Prong bends sharply along the bottom of its slope. There are woods close by the bank on both sides and pastures opening up behind the trees on the right. A little road parallels the creek on that side, and you might consider walking along it if you are in a hurry, because the stream has become very shallow. It continues this way for several hundred yards downstream, but it does have some pretty scenery to reward those that stay by the water.

I once came across a beaver dam a short distance downstream that was built of sticks cleverly mixed with dozens of moderate-sized rocks. Recently I have seen several such dams on half a dozen different creeks. They seem to stand up to the pressures of high water better than those that are made only of sticks, mud, and leaves.

The river splashes in lively runs for seventy-five yards below this dam through an area of striking limestone ledges that are as slippery as any you will come across. Watch your step as you wade here and use your staff to keep from falling. An ATV track fords the river on these ledges and runs downstream, providing a comfortable path where you can walk a little more easily and still look down to enjoy the beauty of the river.

Shallow, flat stretches run ahead of you toward the next ridge, where the stream pulls away to the right side of the valley at a twenty-foot-high dirt bank. There is a flat area atop this bank, and a short distance away you will pass a little cabin that sits in a small clearing overlooking a series of shallow riffles.

This spot, named Hole in the Wall for the hideout of Butch Cassidy and the Sundance Kid, is used as a retreat by the owner of a local flooring mill and his friends. On many summer weekends and during hunting season, you are likely to find people sitting on the cabin's front porch as you walk by.

Two hundred yards away a dirt road runs down the hill alongside the open field beyond the cabin. This is Texas County Road 4490, which drops down the steep slope from Y Highway on a sharp curve to the left about two miles north of the bridge over the South Prong. The rough track parallels the river for a short distance before it crosses to the other side on another good ford composed of flat limestone sheets. From here it leads up a gentle slope toward an attractive old farmhouse that you can see if you walk a few yards away from the water.

Don't be concerned about trespassing; this is a public road. If you kept on past this farm, bearing to the right at the first intersection, you would come to the little community of Arroll, located a short distance north of Mountain View on W Highway west of Highway 17. The ridge above you on the right grows very high and steep beyond the ford. The many rock ledges are often decorated with beautiful flows of ice in cold weather. If you are a hardy enough soul to get out in the winter, it is a wonderful time to enjoy the river.

After a couple of small curves, the river flows a foot or two below some wide, flat ledges that go back twenty or thirty feet from the water. The owner of the farm up the hill can often be found lying peacefully on these ledges, relaxing to the sound of the running water. This is a great spot to stop and let your tensions flow away with the stream. The owner is usually very friendly to hikers who are polite and respect his property.

At the next bend there is sometimes a deep pool, but recently it has silted in until it is only a little over waist-deep. The best hole now is along the right bank below the low ledges around the next curve to the left. The locally uncommon blue lobelia, known in the area as the blue cardinal flower, can be found on this part of the river. One October I found a few blossoms still hanging on even after the first two frosts of the season had dusted the valley. The ridge grows ever higher on the left and is crowned with a thick stand of cedars. There haven't been many good spots to fish for some distance, but don't get discouraged. There are some excellent places ahead.

The ridge gradually tapers off toward a more open area where the river flows wide and shallow around occasional boulders. Soon a primitive road comes down the hill from the right and hits the stream at a wide hole that sometimes has its water deepened by a beaver dam. When the floods leave them alone long enough, the beavers turn a shallow run into a safer home for themselves and, unintentionally, into a great fishing hole. Smallmouth and goggle-eye love the still waters behind the dams.

The road crosses the river and runs down the left side through beautiful stands of oaks and maples. Take the road for a while to enjoy the quiet woods and ready yourself for an uncommon sight. Look to the left when you come to a small gully, where you will see the curving front of a beautiful ledge that sweeps across the channel at the top of a ten-foot-high wall of rock. A small spring drains over this ledge down into a deep hollow at its base. When you get closer, you can see that there is another ledge thirty feet farther upstream that is almost identical to the first. In dry weather the unique double falls are only peaceful trickles, but after the rains begin, they turn into impressive cascades. You can get around to the upstream side of the falls by taking the first turn to the left after the road crosses over the gully.

The narrow lane continues downstream along normally shallow portions of the river and under some high voltage transmission lines. The ridge on the right gets higher and higher until it becomes one of the tallest on the upper river. The road finally curves into the water at the center of a pretty and very long hole where I caught four bass on my last trip downriver.

The channel splits below here, the main branch running long and shallow beneath only moderate slopes on either side. There are a few boulders with some deep water around them where you might find a few fish willing to strike. An attractive rock column pushes out into the stream ahead of you on the left before the next bend.

Beyond this curve the shallow runs gradually slant off into a deep area on the left. A large sycamore tree leans out from the bank about halfway down the long, deep hole. This section has been little changed by flood waters in the past ten years. In warm weather I have seen small gar in the shaded water of this pool, but they don't usually go much farther upstream. Smallmouth a little larger than the average, as well as big goggle-eye, are more common here. There is a cave mouth in the prominence high above the river below the big sycamore.

Around the next bend the largest spring for several miles around pours in from the right, lowering the temperature of the stream noticeably and making the flow wider and deeper. A road adjoining open fields runs above the right bank for half a mile downstream. There are few areas of deep water in this part of the river, and the road is probably the best choice for hiking.

The ridge on the left is steep and high, and County Road 4670, which intersects Y Highway at Low Water, runs back a few yards from its crest. Arroll lies about four miles to the east. As the stream bends to the left around the end of the ridge, there is a long run of deep water where I have caught more goggle-eye than in any other section of the river. An open field runs along the east side of this part of the North Prong, with a deeply rutted dirt lane on its edge that leads over to the gravel road at Low Water.

The high concrete mass and large culverts of the bridge at Low Water come into view ahead as you walk along this pool. The South Prong of Jacks Fork runs along the other side of the promontory to your right, flowing under the three westernmost culverts of the bridge ahead. The two branches of the river unite immediately below the bridge. This is the spot at which you will have left a vehicle if you planned a one-way hike.

When you reach Low Water, be sure to walk downstream for less than half a mile to the outstanding formation known as Chimney Rock. The river is much bigger below the confluence of the two prongs and will be hard to hike along if the water is high. If it is passable, take the left bank around the long curve that runs beneath the high ridge on the south. The big gap in the trees farther down the ridgetop is the right-of-way for the same ammonia pipeline mentioned in chapter 5.

Around the next sharp bend, as the river straightens out to the right and deepens into a charming pool, Chimney Rock towers high above the right bank. A hundred-foot-high column of rock isolated from the cliff behind it, Chimney Rock is a sight well worth seeing and photographing. The climb to its top is not difficult, and the view from that height is terrific.

From there you can see a comfortable-looking cabin standing high atop wooden pilings in the field to the north of the river. These pilings lift it more than fifteen feet above the normal water level of Jacks Fork. Though it may seem hard to believe, I have seen flood waters lapping at the flooring of this cabin after heavy spring rains. That is a good example of the severity of flooding along Ozark streams and should convince you of the danger of camping or parking near the water when there is any chance of thunderstorms. A cave opens high along the downstream side of Chimney Rock. It goes well back into the cliff but is usually very muddy and slippery a short distance from the entrance.

There is a small natural arch a short distance below Chimney Rock that you might be interested in seeing. It stands some six feet high near a large pine tree on the right bank. Hike down the river as far as you wish, but this is usually as far as I go. Fishing generally improves as you hike downstream, except in tourist season, when canoes flood by. At Chimney Rock you have hiked about seven miles, and you still have to go back upstream to Low Water or Kinard Ranch.

MAP 8

South Prong of Jacks Fork,
Little Pine Creek, and Big Pine Creek
(Chapters 11–14)

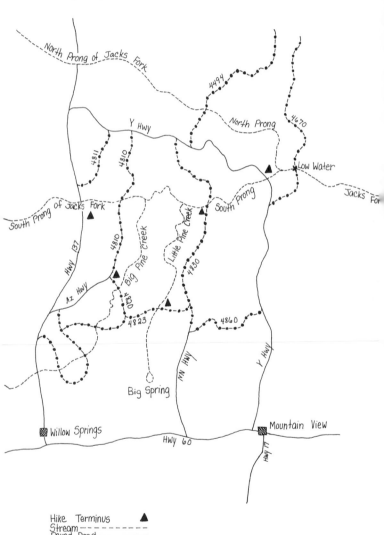

11

Above 4830
(Map 8)

A convenient starting point for several hikes on the South Prong of the Jacks Fork and its tributaries can be reached by traveling north to the end of NN Highway, which lies nine miles east of Willow Springs or seven miles west of Mountain View on U.S. Highway 60. Where the pavement of NN stops, continue straight ahead on Texas County Road 4830 for one and a half miles to a low-water bridge where the clear, rocky stream angles in from the left. The road will narrow and twist on your way down into the valley, but it is always kept in good condition.

There are two parking areas to the left of the road before you get to the stream. The first is down a short dirt lane that leads back into the trees, stopping shy of the gravel bars; it has a handy turnaround a few yards from the water. The second is by the river on the gravel bars near the low-water bridge. There is another low-water bridge over a secondary channel of the river around the next bend in the road and parking spots past this bridge if you find the others filled.

Many people from this area bring their children here in

the summer to swim, but you can usually find a place to park. Those who value solitude on hikes shouldn't be concerned about all the swimmers around the bridges. Very few people get more than one or two hundred yards from road crossings along the river. A few minutes walk from any access point leaves you in a world all to yourself.

If you want to make this a one-way hike, you may park a second vehicle on the north side of the South Prong bridge on Highway 137 north of Willow Springs. Turn east on County Road 4811 north of the bridge and pull quickly back to the right on a little turnoff that leads down to a gravel bar on the river. You may notice that the sign on the bridge refers to this branch of the river as the South Fork of Jacks Fork, but most of the local people and the maps that I use call it the South Prong.

For the first half mile upstream from the low-water bridges, the South Prong flows through a series of deep, still pools and long shallow runs. A long ridge parallels the stream on the south. The deepest pool, another popular swimming hole, is a short distance upstream near the end of the field along the north bank. The ridge above the left bank drops off steeply into the water along most of its length. Hiking in or near the water on that side is next to impossible. A hike up the ridge is interesting, but the old logging road at its crest leads to the back of a private ranch and doesn't follow the river.

A narrow dirt road turns back to the left off 4830 a hundred yards across the river past the second low-water bridge. It leads across the north edge of an overgrown field, then through thick woods until it intersects the river in less than half a mile. If the owners are present and are asked politely, they will probably be willing to allow a hiker to cross their land to the stream, or even to park a vehicle at the end of the road by the river. If there is no one to ask, park by the bridges and stay on the river as you hike.

The property along the north bank of the river above the bridges is owned by a family that plans to build a cabin just above the swimming hole. They don't appreciate strangers on their land who haven't asked permission to cross. There has been a problem between the owners and some thoughtless people who have been dumping garbage near the river, and they are understandably sensitive about their property rights.

After these first deep runs above the low-water bridges, the river winds back and forth for a few hundred yards until it flows between two bluffs. The one along the right bank is much higher and steeper. The bluff on the left is pitted with small caves, most quite shallow, but some show signs of going well back into the rock. About twenty feet above river level on the right, a large cave mouth inevitably draws hikers who pass by to climb up and do a little exploring. The cave consists of one attractive room that tapers off into two dead-end passages at the rear. It offers a cool refuge on a hot summer day and, because of its stable year-round temperature, a comparatively warm shelter for the hardy souls who brave the river in winter.

Upstream from the cave the river makes a ninety-degree turn to the left, with beautiful deep water on the outside of the bend. For several hundred yards above the bend, the river is usually very shallow, having only occasional deep holes around boulders and fallen trees. A small road begins in the gravel bar on the right bank just as the water grows shallow. It crosses the river and divides: one branch goes off into the woods to the left while the other continues up a bar and crosses back over to the right bank. This section of the road parallels the river and goes up to a low-water bridge on Texas County Road 4810 about a quarter of a mile away.

If you prefer to walk up the shaded lane, take a moment to wade a short distance upstream on the river. In the bluff on the left is one of the more unique caves in the area. Watch carefully for the small trail that leads diagonally up the bluff for fifteen or twenty feet to the lower cave entrance. The opening, though large, is almost obscured by foliage in the spring and summer. Inside the cave is a spacious room with a short tunnel to the left and a wide passage up a steep slope to the right. The slope angles up until the floor of the cave gets so near the ceiling that you have to stoop and walk carefully to keep from bumping your head. At no point does the passage close in enough to bother anyone except the particularly claustrophobic. In a few yards the floor slopes back down and you can stand comfortably in another large room at a second opening in the bluff. This cave mouth is even wider than the first and a little higher above the river. There are two small passages that lead from the back of this large room, but they quickly end. There is no safe way down to the river from this opening. Go back through the cave tunnel and down to the river the way you came up.

A little downstream from the low-water bridge on 4810, around the next bend in the river, there is usually a nice pool where the channel swings around to cross under the road. You can probably catch one or two good small-mouth here if there is no one swimming in the deep water. This is another popular swimming area in warm weather. Big Pine Creek joins the river on the outside of this curve before the bridge, draining the beautiful valleys to the southwest. Its flow is a great deal less than that of the South Prong because of its smaller watershed, but it does have its share of deep water and more than its share of unique scenery.

A house sits back a few yards from the river to the left of Big Pine Creek. The lane to the house leads across Big Pine Creek and curves around to intersect 4810 a few yards from its crossing of the river. Signs at the entrance to the little road warn against trespassing. I have never met the owners and would advise the hiker to stay in the streambed when investigating Big Pine Creek. I describe a hike on the creek, along with access points, in chapter 13.

Above the bridge there is a steep ridge on the right that is broken by several small caves, two of which are worthy of your time. To reach either of them requires climbing thirty feet or so up a moderate slope.

The first of these caves consists of a single room extending back a few yards, a snug retreat that I once used to escape heavy rain and lightning during a thunderstorm. The second cave is out of the ordinary. It is a split-level with two separate entrances, one above the other. You have to stoop to get into the lower level, but it is about the same size as the room above. The upper and lower portions of the cave do not appear to be connected at the rear.

In the summer much of the bank and a few of the shallow runs on the South Prong and its tributaries become weedy and overgrown. These areas can be frightening to hikers who are especially concerned about snakes, but reasonable caution will leave little to worry about. There are snakes on this stream and on all others, but most of them are harmless water snakes. They often lie on warm rocks or along the limbs of trees during the day, dropping off into the water at the approach of a hiker. Don't panic and run when you see a snake enter the water, it is only trying to swim away to hide until everything is quiet again. Snakes are shy and they want to keep away from you as much as you want to avoid them; they won't come after you in the water as some people fear.

Wood ducks commonly nest along this part of the South Prong and on many other streams in the Ozarks. It isn't unusual to see a hen and two to six young ducklings paddling up some quiet pool ahead of you in early summer. Don't worry if you see a group of young that seems to have been deserted. The adult ducks shed their primary wing feathers in the summer and are incapable of flying for a few weeks, making them even more shy than usual. The mother is probably hiding nearby, and the ducklings will not wander far in the stream before waddling off into the bushes to hide and wait for her to find them. Sometimes their reluctance to get too far from the hen affords wonderful opportunities to watch them and take pictures. One of my favorite photographs from one summer shows six little balls of fluff that kept swimming around in front of me as unconcerned as if I were a member of the family.

Beyond the first ridge above the 4810 bridge, the river flows through the center of a heavily wooded valley for several hundred yards until it swings over near a high bluff on the left that has several small caves. Two of them seem reasonably deep, but they are too far up a sheer face for the casual climber to reach. A small spring drains down the rock of the bluff a short distance upstream in all but the driest seasons.

The slope drops off abruptly and that side of the river is then bordered by the large pastures of a cattle ranch. Two fences traverse the stream a few hundred yards apart, marking the borders of the ranch. Don't be concerned about crossing the fences, but do be careful around the barbed wire. Above the upper fence a spring branch enters from the right, supplying fully one-third of the river's flow.

For several years I have heard reports of eagles nesting somewhere on the ridges near this spot. I have tried in vain to spot the nest on several trips, but three times I have seen a lone eagle soaring high above me. This seems to lend some substance to the reports of a nest and keeps me coming back to search for it again and again. You should pay more than casual attention to any large, soaring birds circling over the river and learn to tell the difference between eagles and the much more common turkey vultures.

The river becomes quite a bit smaller above this little tributary. There are few pools that are big enough to hold fish until you come to a small bluff on the left. You will find that some of the large rocks in the stream below the bluff have deep water around them. It is fun to check the tops of boulders like these for evidence of the raccoons that are so common here. Many of the rocks are often littered with the shells and claws of large crayfish, the leftovers of raccoon picnics.

Several small spring branches drain into the river from the north above this little bluff. Following them back to their source, you will find they come from a large, spring-fed artificial lake. The lake is impounded behind the high, grassy levee you can see from the bars along the river, but it is completely fenced and you should not cross over the fence for any reason. However, there is a deep overflow pool below the lower end of the levee that you can reach easily from the gravel bars. It is over a hundred feet long and does contain fish.

From this point on, the river is bordered by a wide field on the right, and you can see a house and power lines on the other side of the pasture. This house is on a small county road, Texas County 4811, which intersects State Highway 137 north of Willow Springs in a fourth of a mile.

On the left there is a small bluff, and before you glimpse the green steel of the 137 bridge, you will find there are two more pools that commonly hold large fish. The last hole before you reach the swift run below the bridge is usually very wide and deep. Of course, this depends on the way recent floods have scoured the bottom. Many areas of deep water on small streams shift with the seasons. Deep holes are common along steep bluffs, on the outside of bends, and around boulders and fallen trees, but they may not be precisely where I found them by the time you hike the creek.

In early to mid-June, the last mile of the river valley before you reach the 137 bridge is filled with the delightful smells of many wildflowers and blossoming trees. One of the most obvious and recognizable is the wild pink rose that is so common here. I once discovered, to my great surprise, that another heady, pungent scent comes from a small- to medium-sized tree that is covered with clusters of white bell-like flowers. The flowers droop down beneath heart-shaped leaves, and they are attached to a long, slender, leaflike bract that looks something like a willow leaf. This unusual bract is a sure clue that the tree is a basswood, a member of the linden family. The bract, with the seeds, remains to help you identify the trees later in the year.

The American hop hornbeam is another unusual little tree that grows along the river's edge. It has distinctive winter catkins, often in clusters of three, which develop into flowering catkins in April and May. By June the fruit covers the tree in thick, attractive cascades that bear a striking resemblance to hops—hence the name.

A smaller relative, also growing in this area, is the American hornbeam. It has a smooth-barked, muscular-looking trunk, and its fruit consists of winged seeds that are not so reminiscent of hops. The wood of the American hornbeam is heavy and decay-resistant, and it is often used for long-lasting fence posts. The tree is frequently referred to as ironwood, but is not related to the true ironwood of the tropics. Keep an eye out for these distinctive trees all along the river.

The parking area for the upper terminus of this hike lies on the downstream side of the Highway 137 bridge to your right. The river above this point does contain some fishable water, but it is much less interesting than the stretches below. There are other hikes on more attractive and unusual tributaries back downstream.

12

LITTLE PINE CREEK ══════════

(Map 8, p. 100)

Little Pine Creek is the first tributary of the South Prong that enters from the left above the low-water bridge where County Road 4830 crosses the main stream. The opening of the previous chapter describes the route to the hike terminus at the bridge, as well as parking areas. For this hike the upper parking area on the stream side is preferable because it is closest to the mouth of the creek on the left bank of the South Prong.

The steep ridge to your right as you start upstream parallels the creek for a short distance. This promontory marks the end of the divide between the watersheds of Little Pine Creek and the river. It gradually separates from the creek, as does the ridge up which County Road 4830 climbs to the left, until the stream is flowing down the center of a heavily wooded valley.

The water supply here is meager under normal conditions, and there are few spots that hold large fish. There are some fishable spots, the best of which are backed up by beaver dams, but this hike is most notable for its scenery and wildlife. As you walk along the stream you will see crowds of extra-large tadpoles that swim slowly away from you in almost every pool. These are bullfrog tadpoles, and from the number of them that you see in secluded streams such as this, it may seem a little surprising that the banks aren't lined with row upon row of bullfrogs. But the tadpoles' slowness makes them easy prey for the many birds, animals, and fish that feed on them, and by the time the tadpoles grow up there will be comparatively few of them left as adult frogs.

The little stream wanders back and forth through the valley without offering anything of special interest until, in about three-quarters of a mile, you come to the low-water bridge on Texas County Road 4823. A short distance upstream from the bridge, the channel splits and encircles one of the largest gravel bars you will ever see on so small a creek. At first sight, the bar resembles a cleared field, but its surface is entirely made up of washed gravel and large rocks, with patches of weeds and shrubs that can survive in such an environment scattered across its surface. Unless you pass this spot soon after a flood, the remains of campfires, often within rings of rock, reveal that the area is sometimes used by local hunters and fishermen as a campsite.

There are some small pools above this bar, and they will produce sizable smallmouth, but only for those who are extremely quiet and careful. Little Pine Creek is the perfect example of a tiny stream where you have to be as much a stalker and hunter as a fisherman. If the fish see you and dart away, don't bother to cast; they won't strike after being startled. Larger smallmouth have an annoying habit of rushing from hiding to pursue a smaller fish that you have hooked—sometimes even trying to take the lure from its mouth—before they vanish, never to be seen again. If a fish does strike and avoids getting hooked on your lure, it is not likely that it can be coaxed into striking again. Simply move on and keep the spot in mind for your return trip.

Wild raspberries are common here, their white-coated canes making them easy to identify. They ripen about the middle of June and have the same wonderful, pungent raspberry flavor you have come to expect from domesticated varieties. Their seeds are hard and woody, and if you gather any to use in cooking, avoid things like pies and jams in which the seeds would be a bother. Wild raspberries are great in jellies, syrups, and juices; things that enable you to savor the flavor without suffering the aggravation of the seeds.

Farther upstream a large cliff rises from the left. Much of its surface is obscured in summer by the vegetation, but it is an impressive feature in so confined an area, rising to eighty feet and more above the creek. There are occasional outcroppings of a maroon rock in the creek bed below the bluff that are quite beautiful. Some small cave openings can be seen, but none of any size that are within reach. As is so often the case, the larger caves seem to be on rock faces too steep to be reached easily. As the bluff tapers off on its upstream end, a small spring cascades down the rock and runs into the creek.

Lovely bluffs, with their complement of shallow ledges and caves, alternate from one side of the stream to the other for the next several hundred yards. The creek grows ever smaller as you pass spring after spring and the water supply diminishes. To your right you will soon notice a rather large spring branch entering straight toward you as the creek veers slightly to the left. The branch is choked with watercress, indicating that the cold, mineral-laden water emerges from deep beneath the surface somewhere up ahead.

Follow the branch and you will arrive at one of the most pleasant and charming spots you could hope to encounter after a lengthy, tiring hike. In a long, flat clearing, well above the level of the creek, a comfortable campground has been constructed on a tree-shaded shelf between the base of the hill and a little bluff that drops off into the water. It is complete with a pair of outdoor toilets (marked "Bucks" and "Does"), two small pavilions, a stone barbecue pit, and benches around two of the trees. A little bridge spans the spring branch, and the sign on the far side reads, "Talahatchie Bridge, Load Limit 150." Don't try to cross this old, rotten bridge because its load limit is probably closer to 150 ounces than it is to 150 pounds.

The road above the bridge swings on down the hill and around the upstream end of the campground. It crosses the spring flow on a concrete bridge below the opening in the rocks where the spring emerges from the hillside. A sign on a tree by the creek reveals that this is "Lee's Park, dedicated October 4, 1980," and another sign out on the road denies responsibility for accidents. I have never seen no-trespassing signs around the park, and there seems to be an implied invitation for the weary hiker to stop and rest for a while. Check the signs carefully because things can change over the years, and it could be posted at some time in the future. If you do make use of the area, be careful, because the structures are growing old and a little unsound in spots. It is nonetheless a peaceful place to rest and enjoy the view across the creek while you recuperate from miles of walking. Please respect the rights of the people who went to so much trouble to build the park. Try to leave the spot cleaner than you found it.

The creek above the camp runs gracefully over a series of flat ledges in a long straight section before striking a dark bluff on the right and curving away in a stretch of deep water. Farther up is a large pool behind a usually well-kept beaver dam. For a long distance past this dam, there is little besides shallow, swift water. Occasional springs enter from either side, and there are several more beaver dams, usually in a state of disrepair.

Unless you want to walk for another mile and a half to where the branch from Big Spring enters from the left, this is a good place to end your hike and start back down. If you have the time and the inclination to go on, Big Spring is the largest spring for several miles around and is worth the effort to find it. I have visited the spring many times by hiking down an old logging road, and I seldom go far up the creek beyond Lee's Park. The spring is not in a class with the really large ones on the bigger streams, but it does supply the majority of the flow of upper Little Pine Creek.

13

BIG PINE CREEK ══════════════

(Map 8, p. 100)

Unless you would like to walk up from the 4830 crossing on the South Prong and repeat the lower part of the trip up the river to the mouth of Big Pine Creek (see chapter 11), this trip should start from a low-water bridge farther upstream. Take Texas County Road 4830 north from the end of NN Highway, as on the trip down to Jacks Fork, and turn left on Texas County Road 4823 before 4830 begins its steep descent down to the river. Follow 4823 past the low-water bridge over Little Pine Creek and up the next ridge to its intersection with Texas County Road 4820. Turn right on 4820 to the bottom of the next valley and the low-water bridge over Big Pine Creek. The only parking spot is a narrow area on the right of the road before it crosses the bridge. You must park parallel to the right-of-way.

Those wishing to make this a one-way hike can leave another vehicle at the low-water bridge on Texas County Road 4810. To reach this point, take 4820 past the parking area mentioned in the previous paragraph until the road intersects Texas County Road 4810. Turn right on 4810 and follow it to the next stream crossing, which is the low-water bridge over Jacks Fork. It crosses the river less than fifty yards downstream from the mouth of Big Pine

Creek. Go over the bridge and park on the edge of the wide gravel bar beside the water.

Walking downstream from the bridge on 4820 at the upper end of the hike, you immediately encounter an impressive bluff above the left bank, and a short distance down there is a large cave opening high up on the hillside that can be reached without too much trouble. A large, open field borders the stream for about three hundred yards on the right.

The bluff soon drops away into a more gentle slope with a few rock outcroppings among the dirt and talus. Farther on another bluff leans out over the creek from this same side with an overhanging ledge under its crown at the downstream end. There appears to be a dark opening back under this ledge that the adventuresome hiker could possibly reach by going up on top of the bluff and climbing down around the point where the ledge tapers off into the hillside.

The stream's swift, shallow flow passes beneath these two bluffs, with little, if any, deep water. Below the second bluff on the left, a more heavily wooded cliff towers over the opposite side of the valley, and the creek turns along its rock face. There is a long, deep hole here from which I have consistently caught large bass. This bluff recedes from the stream for a few yards and then returns, with a few cave openings visible high up on its face. After the heights on the right taper off into a long meadow, the land rises into a moderate precipice on the other side. There is some deep water here, especially around a large boulder that has tumbled down from above.

Keep your eyes high on the left bank as you move downstream from this point. You are coming to one of the most impressive features on any small stream in the Ozarks. Arching upward from a point about twenty feet above creek level, a beautiful natural bridge lifts its massive span parallel to the stream. The two buttresses at either end are some forty feet apart at their bases and twenty-five feet apart at the top. The clearance of the thin, flat top of the bridge over the steeply sloping hillside averages about fifteen feet. The center of the bridge is approximately eight feet wide and two feet thick at its thinnest point. Sitting incongruously atop the middle of the span is a boulder weighing several tons that seems bent on collapsing the slender arch beneath it. There is a shallow, round cave at the uphill end of the left buttress, and a deeper vertical crevice leading back into the rock just up from its downhill margin.

This natural bridge, which doesn't seem to be mentioned in any of the reference books I have seen, is more impressive than most. It is not, as many are, just a narrowly separated extension of a cliff face. The uphill side of this arch is open to the trees and sky, and the hillside slopes up beyond the bridge at the same angle as that below. Other bridges are hard to see from a distance and must be visited when the leaves are off the trees to be noticed at all. This beautiful specimen can be seen in any season, but for the best photographs it should be visited in the autumn or winter. It can be reached comfortably in thirty minutes or less of easy walking down the creek.

As you continue your hike below the bridge, the creek winds through a series of bends that contain isolated pockets of deep water. A high, pine-covered ridge stands well above the valley and angles across in front of you farther downstream, deflecting the watercourse to the left along its flank. The streambed below this turn is floored with extremely slippery flat shelves of limestone. Be very careful to avoid falling in areas like this; use a wading staff and keep your steps short and slow, moving forward by sliding your feet carefully ahead without lifting them much above the slick rock. It would only take a second's carelessness to hurt yourself badly.

These ledges end in a beautiful round pool that is one of the deepest and most intensely colored in the entire watershed. The pool is worth a moment's pause to enjoy its peaceful charm, and there are always fish waiting in its translucent green depths. It never fails to surprise me that this has not become a popular swimming hole, since it is only about fifteen minutes' easy hiking from the low-water bridge over the South Prong on Texas County Road 4810. The pools close to the bridge that most swimmers use are far inferior to this. Convenience rather than quality seems to be the major concern in the choice.

Flowing out of the deep hole, the creek tumbles down a series of swift, rocky rapids that empty into a long pool. Though not very deep, it seems to be good for a few fish every time I hike the creek. Farther downstream is a dark bluff on the left, and an open field begins back a few yards from the right bank. There are deep holes along the foot of the bluff that can pay off in good catches if you are patient and quiet.

An electric service line is now visible out in the field to your right. This leads to the house, mentioned in the description of the hike up the South Prong, which stands near Jacks Fork below the confluence of the creek and the river. There is one more beautiful, deep, fish-filled pool downstream, at the end of which you will cross a rather battered low-water bridge on the private road leading to the house on your right. The road is posted, so don't leave the streambed at this point.

Within a hundred yards the creek bends slowly to the right and intersects the South Prong of Jacks Fork in a small pool below the low-water bridge on Texas County Road 4810. This is the spot mentioned at the beginning of the chapter at which you can leave a vehicle for a one-way hike.

Whether or not you intend to walk back upstream to your starting point at the parking area on 4820 to complete your trip, a short hike up Big Pine Creek above the bridge there is worthy of your consideration. Immediately upstream from the 4820 low-water bridge, the creek turns to the right against a beautiful bluff that rises eighty to one hundred feet above the valley floor. Huge, flat rocks that have tumbled from high above litter the streambed, and there are several pools along the curve that harbor respectable fish populations. The creek grows quite shallow as it straightens out above the curve, and the bluff slopes rapidly down until it is no more than a series of ledges barely above the waterline.

A small pool in this straight section of the creek is commonly littered with peeled branches, and the right bank is pierced with several beaver den openings. A quiet person who hides back away from the bank on either side stands a great chance of seeing several beavers as they go about their industrious affairs.

A little spring enters the main stream from the left a few yards upstream. It flows in through a steep, narrow defile and seems to emerge from beneath two large rocks. A moderately high, pine-crested ridge bends the creek back to the left past the spring, where a lovely pool, shading to deep green on the opposite side, slants away from you toward a sheer rock cliff.

In a few yards a steep gully makes its way down the bluff from high above; it is littered with a disgusting array of old car parts, kitchen appliances, and assorted household junk. Dumps like this are getting more rare, but that doesn't make it any less painful to find a beautiful spot despoiled in such a way.

As the creek straightens out above this bend, there are several small areas of deep water against the right bank, but the stream grows more and more shallow as you proceed. In less than a fourth a mile another low-water bridge crosses the creek. This bridge can be reached by turning left instead of right onto 4820 as you come up Texas County Road 4823. Unless you want to leave a car at that bridge, or just have plenty of time, there is little reason to hike that far upstream. Your time could be better spent on the next hike down the South Prong.

14

SOUTH PRONG OF JACKS FORK ═══════════

Downstream to Y Highway
(Map 8, p. 100)

Downstream from Texas County Road 4830 is another hike on the South Prong of Jacks Fork that runs four to six miles to Y Highway. It can be made one-way by leaving a vehicle at the public parking area below the Y Highway bridge, six miles north of Mountain View. Mountain View lies east of Willow Springs, about six miles east of the turnoff on NN that leads to the upper sections of the river.

The parking spot on Y Highway can also be reached by continuing across the low-water bridges over the South Prong on 4830 to its intersection with the highway about three miles away. Turn right on Y until it dips down into the river valley in approximately four miles. The parking area is on the east side of the bridge on a large gravel bar. It is closed to public use after ten o'clock at night. Use the same spots along 4830 that are described in chapter 11 for parking at the upper end of this hike.

Below the first of the two low-water bridges over the divided South Prong, the river runs narrow and swift over flat, slippery rock ledges with a ridge climbing steadily above the valley's right margin. There is a miniature waterfall over a shallow ledge across this branch before the other channel of the river rejoins the main stream from the left. The amount of water in the two channels varies, but in recent years the left branch has been growing smaller, and the shorter, more direct curve of the right channel has taken an increasing share of the river's flow.

Past the junction there is a long, wide pool with a good population of smallmouth that is often missed by impatient fishermen because there is hardly any really deep water here. A bit of quiet caution can bring surprising results in spots like this. I have had three people tell me they have seen river otters in this pool, but I can't confirm from personal experience that they are there. On several trips I have spotted a small, beaverlike animal swimming back and forth across the pool ahead of me, but it has always disappeared into a den under a sycamore on the left bank before I could get close enough to identify it. The animal seems too small for an adult beaver, and I haven't found any beaver cuttings or peeled limbs on the bank anywhere along the pool. My skill at identifying footprints and other signs on the shore isn't sufficient to prove anything one way or the other. The Missouri Department of Conservation has released otters at other points on Jacks Fork, but besides beavers there are muskrats on some of our streams that could be confused with them. Bring your binoculars and make the search for otters another reason for hiking Jacks Fork.

The river now turns to the left and runs past a small valley with a dirt lane that follows it off to the right into private lands. Along the next bluff downstream, deep water extends completely across the stream. When the water is low enough, you can walk past this point along the ledges at the foot of the bluff. If the river is too high, you will have to leave the stream temporarily and hike along the left bank.

The branch that drains Stillhouse Hollow comes in from the right beyond this bluff, and the little valley through which it flows offers a fascinating detour that you should not miss. Everything in the hollow is on an intimate, reduced scale, and it remains dark, cool, and secluded even on hot summer days. This little tributary flows through a cavelike canopy of trees for a few yards off the river until an open field appears on the right. Upstream of the field, a small road comes down to the creek. Follow the road to the right when you first intersect it, and you will come to the foundations of an old house set back against the base of the hill.

You can keep going upstream along this road for a while instead of wading up the creek if you want to take advantage of the more even surface. This lane runs along the creek bed for a short distance through small spring pools, and it crosses the stream in a washed-out drop-off that would seem to bar all but small ATVs from driving past.

To the right of the road, up from the point it crosses the stream, is an impressive three-trunked butternut tree. Butternuts this large are hard to find because most big trees have been cut for their beautiful, light-colored wood. Their bark looks a lot like that of black walnut with whitish highlights, and in fact, the trees are sometimes called white walnuts. The nuts of this tree ripen in the fall and have an unusual sweet flavor. Treat yourself to the taste of a butternut if you come across one of the trees at the right time of year. The nuts don't keep well, souring very quickly unless the meats are frozen. Don't gather too many of them unless you plan to use them or freeze them right away.

A short distance ahead, the lane dead-ends in a more-traveled dirt road. Bear to your right up this county road until it hits the creek, and walk up the creek bed for the rest of your hike up the hollow. For a few hundred yards there is nothing but heavy woods along the stream, and then you come to two lovely bluffs along the left bank. The bluffs are not large and probably wouldn't attract your attention in a more open setting, but they are in perfect proportion with their small-scale surroundings.

The first bluff is covered with cascades of delightful maidenhair ferns, which grow thickly in this damp, sheltered part of the valley. A spring trickles slowly down the rock face, dripping gently into a small pool below. In the summer this spot has a tropical atmosphere. The upper bluff has an overhanging ledge at its top and is attractive in its own right, with several kinds of ferns clinging to its surface and growing along the stream bank. The space beneath the overhang is deep enough to offer some protection if you should be caught in a storm. Spring branches trickle in occasionally from either side as you walk past this point, and shortly you will come to a fence across the creek, marking the boundary of the wooded section of a large pasture. Beyond the fence attractive rock ledges underlie the stream, which flows over them in a succession of small cascades.

Look upstream as you pass these ledges to see ahead of you a higher ledge over which the water tumbles in a near vertical drop of about eight feet. The entire width of the ledge in the streambed is some fifteen feet, but there is seldom an unbroken flow from one bank to the other. This little waterfall is among the most pleasing sights I have ever encountered, coming so unexpectedly as it does after a mile-long hike up such a gently sloping valley.

Make certain you have your camera with you to take pictures of the falls. This spot has different faces in different seasons, and no one photograph can do it justice. Beyond the falls is a ford on a road that passes through the pasture, and another stretch of small ledges across the stream. There is little reason to go any farther than the upper limits of this series of drop-offs.

Back on the South Prong the river assumes the character it keeps more or less uniformly for the next three miles down to Y Highway. It swings gradually back and forth across a wide valley with expansive gravel bars on one or both sides. There are only a few deep holes where the stream runs against isolated rock faces. The next pool lies upstream of a big open pasture with a barn on its upper fringe, and it is the longest and deepest for miles. This giant hole runs against the hills on the north side of the valley for over two hundred yards. Take your time to enjoy this spot and fish it carefully. There are more fish here than in any pool for the next two or three miles. The pool is full of goggle-eye, and fishermen using live bait seem to make the best catches here. A small utility line crosses the river below the pool.

Farther downstream, there are some rock outcroppings with deep water beneath them before the river straightens out in a long run through big gravel bars. At the end of this straight and shallow portion of the creek, a house sits back in the trees to the left. The spot is referred to as "Hattie" on detailed contour maps. The house lies at the end of Texas County Road 4850, which leads to Y Highway about a mile to the north.

The river now crosses completely across the valley to the south side and tumbles through a straight, swift section where deer frequently cross. It is not unusual to see deer standing in the water along here, eyeing you as you wade in that direction. For some reason, they seem less shy when both you and they are in the river.

This shallow flow runs into a deep pool along the small bluff at its lower end. The river farther down has only two more small pools before the bridge over Y Highway. This entire area of the river valley is the object of extensive gravel-digging. The tracks of heavy machinery and trucks are visible everywhere, and sometimes it is hard to walk through the holes and piles of gravel that dot the bars.

A large power line crosses the river before the last bluff above the bridge. Cross under the bridge and you are at the end of your hike at the parking area on Y Highway. This is only three hundred yards above the spot where the North Prong and South Prong of Jacks Fork unite at a low-water bridge to form the main stream of the lower river. The bridge and the area around it are simply referred to as "Low Water" by the people who live in the area. Canoeing is extremely popular downstream from this access point on the river. Many canoe rental services are available in the region and are easy to locate by asking about them at any local store. A trip down the North Prong is described in chapter 10.

MAP 9

Noblett Creek–Spring Creek

(Chapters 15–18)

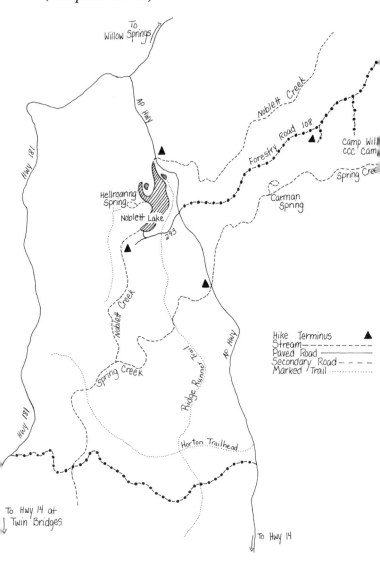

15

NOBLETT CREEK ═══════════════

Above Noblett Lake
(Map 9)

      Noblett Creek is an attractive stream that flows through a deep, narrow valley filled with gushing springs and rocky bluffs. About a mile below the bridge where it crosses under AP Highway, the stream is backed up into a lovely twenty-eight-acre lake. Noblett Lake is impounded behind a dam built by CCC (Civilian Conservation Corps) workers at Camp Willow in the 1930s (for more on Camp Willow, see chapter 16). Two miles below the dam and its well-developed camping and picnic areas, Noblett Creek and Spring Creek join, flowing off toward the North Fork of the White River several miles away.

From Willow Springs, take State Route 76 west for eight miles from the caution light at the Highway 60 intersection. Turn left on State Route 181 and go south for two miles to AP Highway. Just before you reach AP, look for the dirt road, Howell County 283, turning to the right beyond Blue Buck Church. It leads to the Blue Buck fire tower scenic overlook. A few yards down the small road, the tower offers a lovely view of heavily wooded hills rolling away to the horizon in every direction.

Take AP south from Highway 181 for about three miles to the bridge over Noblett Creek, just north of the road to

Noblett Lake. There are parking places at either end of the bridge on the east side of the highway, the north area being larger and more open.

Throughout most of its course, the watershed of Noblett Creek parallels that of Spring Creek, the two being separated by a long, wide ridge down the top of which runs Forestry Road 108 between AP and Howell County Road 560. It is advisable to make the hike from AP up Noblett Creek a one-way excursion, since it is longer than most described in this book. With an average amount of sight-seeing and fishing, this trip should take about six hours.

The endpoint for this hike up Noblett Creek is near the Camp Willow starting point for the hike down the upper portion of Spring Creek. To reach Camp Willow, turn left off AP onto Forestry Road 108 and proceed three and a half miles. Go a few hundred yards to the east of Camp Willow, turning at the first small road to the left, just a few yards beyond the stone columns on either side of the main road. One vehicle can be left parked in front of the barrier on this overgrown lane. If you must walk back to the bridge, return by way of the forestry road to eliminate the difficult twists and turns of Noblett Creek. One useful strategy if you don't have a second vehicle is to leave a bicycle parked at the endpoint and cycle back down to AP, since the road is primarily downhill in that direction.

If you have time before beginning the hike upstream, you should take advantage of an interesting little diversion of about two hours that awaits you below the bridge. This side trip leads down the creek for half a mile and then along a well-marked trail around the upper part of Noblett Lake to the rather aptly named Hellroaring Spring.

Hellroaring Spring

Below the bridge on AP the creek turns slightly left, having deep water on the outside of the bend and to the right of the straight section at its end. The next curve, a wide oxbow, is nothing more than a big loop of shallow water that you can cut off by going straight across its neck. The slope of the north bank becomes steeper beyond the curve, and the stream narrows around several large boulders that have tumbled down the hill into the water. After a gentle arc to the left, the creek is nearly blocked with fallen rock, and a slight ledge protrudes from the right bank above a deep pool of water. Another group of large rocks at the end of the hole contains more pockets of deep water.

Downstream of the rocks is a shallow run with a quick left-right curve, after which the water narrows and turns slightly to the right, opening into a nice pool along a steeper slope. Just before this next pool, the Ridge Runner Trail (a long trail that runs for several miles around Noblett Lake and eventually to the White River) crosses the creek, its path marked on either side with brown Forestry Service signs. The sign on the left is more easily visible, the sign on the right being hidden by tall weeds in the summer. If you are interested in fishing them, there are two more good pools before the creek widens out into the lake beyond the trail crossing.

To reach Hellroaring Spring, take the trail to the right. The path is marked frequently with gray, diamond-shaped guides nailed to the trees. Quite well worn and easy to follow, it is often used by people on horseback. Follow the trail up the side of the ridge to its crest, climbing past the projecting rocks through which it winds near the top. Pace yourself if you are not in good physical condition, because the trail is very steep in spots.

The trail intersects an old logging road atop the ridge and then winds down the other side, dividing into two branches beside a small spring branch at the bottom. One fork crosses the little stream, and the other continues on down the left bank. Take the left fork through a large stand of May apples. Their fruit reaches golf-ball size by late June, ripens later in the summer, and is used by many to make a delicious jelly. The trail crosses the stream in a few yards and starts up the ridge on the far side, where it rejoins the other loop.

Follow the trail past this intersection to the point at which a small spring flow comes across from the right. Walk to the left down this branch to its juncture with the main stream. At times the larger branch has gone underground here. The two streams meet in an attractive area of rock ledges over which they tumble on their way to the lake. Follow the flow of the water downstream to your right.

When the channel divides, if you stay on the branch of the creek that hugs the left side of this small valley, you will not come out at the spring, but you will discover some trees that are unusual for a spot this far north in the Ozarks. As the woods thin out near the lake, there are four bald cypress trees growing off to the right of the channel. The largest of these is about a foot in diameter and twenty-five to thirty feet tall. This cypress is an unusual conifer that sheds its tiny needles in the fall and is much more at home in southern swamps, where some specimens have reached heights of one hundred twenty feet and a diameter of six feet or more.

To reach the spring, stay on the right side of the valley and follow the clear, roadlike area that leads off to the right as the channel splits. This branch of the streambed above the spring may be dry in the summer. When the water table is high, you can tell from well upstream how Hellroaring Spring got its name. The sound of its rushing flow from the hillside can carry for a considerable distance through the quiet woods.

Upon reaching the spring, you will find that it gushes out from twin openings in the rocks on the right bank of the channel. It drops over a small ledge in a noisy, splashing fall that drains off into Noblett Lake, only about fifty yards away. The lake in this spot is very shallow, having a mucky bottom that makes wading out to fishable water next to impossible. To take the hike upstream from AP, retrace your path from the spring back up to the bridge.

Noblett Creek above AP Bridge

The stretch of Noblett Creek immediately above the bridge over AP is characteristic of the streams flowing through this region. The extensive layers of sedimentary rock capping the ridges and lining large areas of the streambed give rise to high bluffs, as well as numerous flat ledges and caves. Less than two hundred yards upstream, the ridge on the right bank is crowned with a series of deep, overhanging ledges that continue intermittently up to the next large bend to the left. These ledges and the ones around the upstream bend on the other side of the creek are ideal protection during thunderstorms.

Never wade in streams when you see lightning flashing or hear thunder rolling over the nearby ridges. The deadly effects of a lightning strike can carry for great distances through the mineral-laden water. Take shelter in caves or dry overhanging ledges such as these whenever possible. Make certain that you stay high above the water level during a storm, for this stream and many others like it have been known to rise several feet in a few minutes during heavy rains. Don't get into a position where rising water might cut off the escape routes from your refuge.

One recent spring afternoon, I had to climb up a hazardous overhang because a flash flood rose above the trails at both ends of the ledge I was hiding under during a thunderstorm. It wasn't the safest thing in the world to do, but it was either that or wait for the water to go down. Darkness was coming on, and I didn't relish walking out through the steep valley after sunset. I learned a lesson that afternoon, and I hope you can profit from my experience.

Above the winding curves beyond the ledges is a long, straight flow that leads toward a high ridge standing perpendicular to the creek. The immediate locale seems to be a common nesting ground for a large number of mourning doves. Their sorrowful cooing fills the air along this part of the stream all summer long. Noblett Creek turns along the ridge ahead and goes to the right in a shallow riffle past a little valley to the north. Beyond the valley, the ridge returns to a point near the stream and gradually gives way to a more gentle slope with a fine pool at its base.

After a right-angle turn, the water remains swift and shallow until you reach a gentle curve to the left. Around this bend is a long, impressive pool with a rocky slope on its south bank that gets progressively steeper as you go upstream. Some small caves dot the upper end of the bluff, and the bank remains steep and rocky for a great distance ahead. After a lengthy stretch of water with few if any deep holes, the creek bends sharply north into the center of the valley, far away from any rocky outcroppings. A large beaver dam usually deepens the creek in this area, where untold numbers of wood ducks have been raised. Look into any trees that lean out over the creek for these gaudy little ducks, who perch among the branches. They nest in tree hollows, from which the young flutter down to the water below when they are ready to leave the nest.

There is another lengthy, shallow series of bends and riffles ahead. When you come to a large field on the left after passing a little spring branch, you will find that a beaver dam at the upper end of the field backs up a very deep pool over a hundred fifty yards in length. To fish the pool and avoid the tangled growth on the north bank in summer, walk along the steeper slope to the right.

Through the shallows above, there are several bends in the creek well away from the bluffs on either side. The floor of the channel consists of heavily fissured layers of multicolored rock that make an unusually beautiful streambed. These rock beds are not as slippery as many others along the way, but you should still exercise care in crossing them.

Upstream, a long series of deep rock ledges stands some six feet over the water on the right. These ledges end where a large boulder sits on the right of the creek. Curving, shallow rapids continue above the boulder until a slough enters from the right at a sharp turn to the left.

Deep water continues up from this point along a twenty- to twenty-five-foot bluff as the creek swings around to run parallel to its base.

One of the deepest, most beautiful overhangs along any creek adorns the upstream end of this bluff. The stream flows completely back under a dark cavity where the rock hangs so far out over the creek that it seems to be doing its best to defy the law of gravity. The bluff slopes down near water level as the creek turns toward the south wall of the valley in a series of shallow bends and runs. It straightens out against small ledges and bluffs on the right, then winds back and forth between gently sloping banks until a long pool opens up against another steep bluff. A gravel bar extends well back under the bluff in a shelf wide enough to walk along. Small springs seep out from between boulders at water level, and several little caves appear in the rock face above.

Upstream of this small bluff is a yellow sign on a red post a short distance above the water on the right. The sign reads "Property Boundary, National Forest" and marks the edge of the Carman Springs Area, which extends for miles to the south beyond Camp Willow and through the Spring Creek watershed.

Leave Noblett Creek at this point and climb the steep slope to your right, turning up through a little draw to the top of the ridge. You may have to walk a little farther upstream to find a clear enough area on the bank to walk comfortably, but do not go on around the end of the ridge to the east. On the ridgetop ahead you will see a large field. Bear to the right when you see this open area and walk around its perimeter well back in the woods. Don't try to cross the field, as it is virtually impassable, being littered with thousands of limbs and small tree trunks left over from a clear-cutting timber operation.

As you reach the south side of the open area, you will pass a small stand of pines that have been left standing out in the clear-cut. Walk on through another grove of pines at the edge of the woods and you will reach the little logging road that goes back over to Forestry Road

108 near the rock pillars at Camp Willow. Take this little road to the right out to 108.

Pick up your second vehicle if you left it here off the main road or walk back down 108 to AP and the Noblett Creek bridge. Watch for deer and turkey if you do walk this stretch of road; they are extremely common here.

16

SPRING CREEK ══════════════════

Carman Spring to AP Highway
(Map 9, p. 124)

       Spring Creek is a popular name for streams in the Ozarks, but considering the abundance of clear, cold springs that send their waters flowing through valley after valley, it's a wonder we don't have more Spring Creeks than we do. I have hiked and fished six nearby creeks by that name, and two of them are distinctive enough to be included in this book. The Spring Creek near Noblett Lake, south of Willow Springs, runs through what are perhaps the most sparsely settled valleys along any of these streams with the same name. Most of its upper reaches are bordered by the public lands of Carman Springs Wildlife Area, where the fishing can be especially good at times. As you might well imagine, wildlife is everywhere.

From Highway 181 follow AP for four miles to Forestry Road 108, which branches off to the left opposite the entrance to the Noblett Lake Recreation Area. A drive down to the lake and its beautiful dam is certainly worth your while. Noblett Lake is a twenty-eight-acre gem set in a lovely, narrow valley a mile to the east of AP. Its shores offer picnic and camping facilities, and the hills surrounding the lake are crossed by miles of well-marked trails with interesting hikes of various lengths. Check the bulletin board at the trailhead on the Noblett Lake Road for information about the trails. Two of the hikes down the Spring Creek watershed involve a portion of the trail below Noblett Lake, hikes described in chapters 17 and 18.

To reach your starting point for this hike, turn left off AP onto Forestry Road 108. Follow it for three and a half miles until you come to the Camp Willow parking area at the site of the old CCC camp. Forestry service signs identify the area and offer a brief description of the camp and its history.

If you plan to take a leisurely one-way hike, you can leave one vehicle at the bridge over Spring Creek. This bridge is on AP, about one mile south of Forestry Road 108. Turn off to the right before you come to the bridge and park under the large sycamore tree near the creek. If you are going to make this a round-trip and plan to walk back up to the spot where you began, you can choose to return by the roads, AP and 108, or by the creek, depending on the time you wish to spend. It is imperative that you begin the hike at the upstream end, however, because thick undergrowth makes it very hard for those unfamiliar with the area to find their way up the proper ridge to the Camp Willow parking area.

Camp Willow was one of many CCC (Civilian Conservation Corps) camps built in the 1930s to train unemployed men in useful trades. In return for the minimum of ten hours a week of educational and vocational classes, the Corps members were set to work on many projects beneficial to the area. Among the achievements of those at Camp Willow were planting acres of pine trees, building fire towers like that at Blue Buck, fighting fires, reestablishing depleted deer and turkey populations, and constructing the dam at nearby Noblett Lake.

At its prime the camp must have been quite impressive. There were at least eighteen buildings, and the sturdy foundations of many of them still dot the thickening woods. In addition to the facilities one would have expected, there was a croquet court, a weather station, a greenhouse, and a large rock-lined swimming pool, which seems in good enough condition to be used today. Take the time to look around Camp Willow and let your imagination wander through the past.

When you are ready to begin your hike to the creek, follow the old road that leads south and west along the ridgetop through the CCC camp. At the end of the ridge the roadway becomes faint and hard to follow, but continue straight down the steep slope into the valley of Spring Creek. You should intersect the creek a short distance above the point where Carman Spring bubbles from the base of the ridge on the north side of the valley. It splashes its way through a thick mass of watercress before flowing down a small branch to join the main stream a few yards away.

The valley at this point is heavily wooded and narrow, and steep, high ridges line the meandering course of the creek. Many species of hardwood trees native to this part of the state are common here. An observant hiker can find varieties of oak, walnut, hickory, ash, butternut, elm, maple, birch, and more. If you are here in April, look for the hundreds of buckeye trees raising their yellow flower spikes all over the valley floor near the creek. There are frequent patches of cane and occasional overgrown fields filled with wild garlic, blackberries, and the white frosted canes of wild raspberries.

The rich and varied food supply of the region supports a tremendous wildlife population. Deer, turkeys, beavers, quail, squirrels, woodchucks, and rabbits are there for the silent hiker to enjoy. It is unlikely that you would see one, but black bear wander through this region in increasing numbers as they overflow from areas in Arkansas where they have been reintroduced in recent years. One adult bear was killed illegally near Noblett Lake by a thoughtless, trigger-happy hunter in the fall of 1990. Others have been seen all the way from the Arkansas line to the Jacks Fork watershed north of Mountain View and Willow Springs. I have tracked bear through the winter snows across my twenty acres near Sims Valley Lake nearly every winter for the last nine years, but I have never actually seen one there. I did happen upon a half-grown cub three years ago along a gravel bar near the intersection of Little Pine Creek and Jacks Fork. If you should come upon a black bear here or anywhere else in the woods, don't be too frightened. Unless cornered and threatened while defending their young, they will give way to humans—they are as frightened of you as you are of them.

Spring Creek is quite small this far up toward the headwaters. Few people fish here, but there are many small pockets of deep water and a few really big holes that contain sunfish, largemouth, smallmouth, and a fish I used to think of as the rock bass. I have since learned that the fish my friends and I have been calling by that name are either shadow bass or Ozark bass. Goggle-eye is a name that would apply to all three species, but the true rock bass is a native of streams on the northern border of this area. One of the Missouri Department of Natural Resources pamphlets on fish identification or a good book on fish species may prove helpful in identifying your own catch.

To be successful in catching fish here and on any small stream you must be as much a hunter as a fisherman. Stalk the pools slowly and quietly, refraining from sudden motions. If you are wading, take short steps without lifting your feet high off the bottom. Avoid splashing at all costs. Use ultralight equipment and small lures. The fish are there waiting for anyone careful enough to defeat their natural wariness, which is intensified in such close quarters.

Lures such as small jigs and beetles, plastic crawfish, and artificial minnows and worms are usually effective, but more and larger fish are caught on live bait. The waters are full of crawfish and small, slow, minnowlike fish called sculpins. They are easy to catch in the rocky shallows using a little nylon dip-net like the ones many fishermen use to get minnows out of a bucket.

Fish the live bait below a small bobber, with only a split shot or two for weight, at a depth suitable for the stretch of water you are fishing. When there is current enough, let the bait drift quietly downstream ahead of you. If the water is very deep and fishing with the bobber doesn't get results, try fishing on the bottom without a float. Feeding fish constantly cruise the pools and shallows in search of food, so don't be impatient. The fish will come to you if you wait.

For several hundred yards below Carman Spring, the creek is small and unimpressive. It runs through a wide and heavily wooded valley which is littered with a tremendous amount of debris that has washed against rocks and timber, an obvious testimony to the height of flood waters in the rainy season. The stream below the spring runs more or less straight with only a few spots against the ledges and fallen trees that could hold fish. It then angles sharply to the left against a dark bluff in a beautiful, deep hole that is one of the two largest pools on the creek for the next three or four miles. The water against the large bluff drops off into translucent green depths that are often the hiding place of many good-sized largemouth bass.

This pool is deepened by a small dam of rocks around the curve at its lower end. The dam is made even higher with branches piled there by the beavers living along this part of the stream. Dams such as these were built by farmers of the area during the droughts of the 1930s to insure a more stable water supply. Some men even brought their families and livestock down to the streams to survive severe droughts when the springs and shallow wells near their houses dried up in the hottest part of the summer. Many of the small streams in this part of the Ozarks have one or more dams much like this one along their upper reaches. Others were built farther downstream on Spring Creek, but the greater water flow during periods of flooding has washed them away over the years. Even this small dam is being slowly lost to the ravages of floods. If the beaver dam weren't built on top of its remains, I would have had difficulty finding it on my last trip downstream.

Below this pool the creek turns back to the right in a long run, lined by a steep bank on the left that is riddled with the holes of beaver dens. The slope is marked by several well-worn trails up the hill that are made by beaver on their food-gathering expeditions. Some trails extend from the water far into the underbrush. It is easy to pay more attention to the creek at this spot than to where you are putting your feet, and you can easily slip on the muddy trails or step into one of the leaf-covered exit holes of a beaver den if you don't watch where you are going. Keep an eye on your path and probe suspicious, leaf-covered spots with your wading staff.

An interesting little valley leads away to the left as the main stream bends to the right. The rocky bluff that has intruded against the creek for over a hundred yards falls away precipitously at the valley entrance. You can see back into its depths when the trees are bare, but it is screened completely by the dense foliage from the last days of April through the end of October.

A few yards back from the creek, the narrow valley ends in a fifteen-foot-high ledge, forming a miniature box canyon. In wet weather an intermittent stream drops over the ledge in a lovely fall, but it is dry most of the year. The ledge has enough of an overhang to offer protection from the elements, and it is easy to visualize other hunters and fishermen tending their campfires beneath its protection back through the years. It is the discovery of intimate spots like this that can turn ordinary hikes into memorable excursions.

On the bluff a little upstream of this spot and on the last bluff downstream before the bridge at AP, one of the rarer wildflowers in Missouri will be in bloom from early May to mid-June. Watch carefully for the large pink and white blooms of the showy lady's slipper along the moist ledges above the creek. This terrestrial orchid has large, lilylike leaves often as much as two feet high. Please don't pick the blossoms or dig the plants. They are very uncommon, but if that is not reason enough for you to leave them alone, contact with the plants is said to trigger a reaction similar to that caused by poison ivy. Be fore-warned.

Throughout the area below the box canyon, there are many small holes and wide runs, often containing impressive fish. Largemouth up to three pounds and more are not uncommon when the water is high. After several winding turns the stream comes up against another large rock bluff and bears left against its base. Downstream, a portion of a ledge from thirty feet up the bluff has fallen into the water and lies slanting off into the depths. The currents have scoured out deep pockets around and behind this large, tilted intrusion.

One May I found a large red oak that had been undercut by flood waters tumbled into the stream below the fallen ledge. I was mildly surprised to see that beaver had stripped the bark from dozens of the smaller twigs and limbs, leaving the still-green leaves scattered all over the bank. It is more common to find beaver nibbling on sycamore, willow, alder, and cottonwood, but they will eat the tender young branches of practically any tree when nature makes them as easy to get to as this red oak was.

After a few more bends that contain several fishable pockets, the creek turns sharply left against a bluff with a most impressive overhang. In places it leans out as much as twelve to fifteen feet over the rock bank that runs along its base. Hikers passing this point commonly yield to the temptation of crossing over to walk under the bulk of the overhang to enjoy the closeness of the rock.

Walking under the ledge is like passing through some giant tunnel that has been sheared in two lengthwise. It is especially peaceful and satisfying to sit back against the dripping rock and look out across the pool below while you sip water from your canteen and enjoy a snack. This pool is the second of the two largest holes on the upper creek, and it stretches for a hundred yards along and downstream of the ledge. There are a few shallow caves that pierce the bluff upstream of the big overhang. The two with the largest openings are about four feet high and ten feet wide; they extend back only a few yards into the rock. Some of the smaller caves seem to go back a great deal farther.

I once hiked this section of Spring Creek late in the winter with a friend. While I was lazily absorbed in the beauty of the overhang on the lower bluff, my companion was checking out the little caves at its upper end and detected an overpowering musky smell coming out of the deepest cave. We were smart—and scared—enough to keep from intruding any deeper into the cave, but we guessed that some large animal was using it as a den.

I went back a few weeks later to fish the creek in warmer weather and found tracks in the dirt around the cave mouth that made it obvious a fair-sized bear had made the cave its home during the winter. Bear tracks are easy to identify because they resemble prints of small human feet with only four toes.

Farther downstream, the creek meanders back and forth for about half a mile through a series of bends with some deep water on the outside of the curves. The banks here are covered by thick groves of papaws. Common all along Spring Creek, these trees are especially prevalent in this region. The papaw is a small tree, rarely over twenty feet tall, that frequently grows in dense stands because of its habit of sending up suckers from its roots. Its flowers are a unique brown-purple and they appear in the spring before or along with the first leaves. The trees are easily recognized by their large, smooth leaves, which are up to twelve inches long. The fruit ripens in September and resembles a short, fat banana. It has a unique, pungent flavor that is appreciated by opossums, raccoons, and squirrels—and the few humans who have been persistent enough to acquire an appreciation for the taste.

If you are wading this, or any stream, from April through July, be careful of the many conical depressions and piles of small rocks in shallow water. They are the nests of spawning fish. It is easy to avoid them if you are alert and watch your step. Most Ozark streams still have healthy fish populations, and they will stay that way with a little help.

A quarter mile above the bridge over AP, Spring Creek turns sharply to the right and runs straight to the highway in splashing riffles and shallow runs with little deep water anywhere. A small bluff borders the left of the stream, and its upper end is covered with wildflowers in the spring, including the showy lady's slipper. There is a small cave in the bluff just above the bridge that is just deep enough to offer shelter in bad weather. Pass under the bridge and climb the bank toward the large sycamore on the right side. Your second vehicle should be waiting nearby if you have made this a one-way hike.

A leisurely trip down the creek from Camp Willow to the bridge will take approximately three to four hours, depending on the amount of fishing and sight-seeing you do. A return trip at a steady pace will take about half that long, less than that if you go back by way of the roads. If you would like to go farther down Spring Creek, see chapters 17 and 18.

17

THE NOBLETT CREEK/
SPRING CREEK/
RIDGE RUNNER TRAIL LOOP ═══

(Map 9, p. 124)

A short, easy hike along attractive portions of Noblett Creek, Spring Creek, and a mile of the Ridge Runner Trail awaits you at the end of County Road 293 off AP Highway. Turn off Highway 181 onto AP Highway and go four miles to the entrance of the Noblett Lake Recreation Area at Howell County Road 293. Turn to the right off the asphalt road at the sign to Noblett Lake.

When you reach the lake, park by the dam and take some time to enjoy the beauty of the spillway area before beginning your hike. The dam was built in an extremely narrow section of Noblett Creek valley, an ideal spot to form a lovely lake with a minimum of effort. The steep bluffs along the spillway and the stream below are some of the prettiest in the watershed.

Thousands of fish migrate upstream to the base of the dam in early spring and congregate in the deep hole there, much to the delight of local fishermen. The bass season is closed in the streams then, but the pool contains enough bluegill, sunfish, and goggle-eye to satisfy anyone. Fishing is good in Noblett Creek throughout the spring and summer, but the number of fish in the stream tails off in late fall, as they return to the deeper waters downstream. Still, Noblett Creek maintains a steady flow of water and a fair fish population in its three-mile run below the dam even in the driest seasons. Every time I have been there, it has always had a number of deep pools where you can pick up a few fish. On the other hand, Spring Creek, which Noblett joins in a few miles, often shrinks to a trickle above their junction and has hardly any fish in its infrequent shallow holes. It seems unfair that the stream formed by the union of the two is called Spring Creek when it is so much smaller than Noblett Creek throughout most of the year. But who knows how the naming came about?

When you are ready to continue on your way, drive down the road below the dam to the first parking area along the creek. Leave your vehicle in this spot to start your walk down the creek. A large spring gushes out a few yards upstream, on the edge of the woods past the picnic table and cooking facilities. This well-kept campground has all the facilities campers need to make their stay here comfortable and enjoyable. The numbered camping spots require a fee and can be reserved ahead of time to insure their availability. Check the signs on the bulletin boards for more information.

I always begin this hike here and walk it counterclockwise because going in that direction leaves me with an easy downhill section of paved road at the end of the trip. When I am tired after six miles of trails and streams, I don't relish struggling uphill to my truck. The uphill portion of the Ridge Runner Trail is a much gentler slope than the one you would have to face on a clockwise circuit, having tired yourself out at the very beginning on the steep hill up the asphalt road from the lake. Don't come here to hike in deer or turkey seasons. As a matter of fact, it is too dangerous to hike anywhere in the Ozarks during these hunting seasons. The whole region is hunted extensively, and this area is especially popular. All the camping spots are full then, and hunters are everywhere.

Go fishing on a lake to enjoy the outdoors during these times if you don't care to hunt.

This entire campground is under water when it floods, sometimes three feet and more over the pavement; note the sign along the road that aids drivers in judging water depth when the creek is out of its banks. A loop of the Ridge Runner Trail crosses above this sign and goes across the creek to join the main trail along the top of the ridge to the west. The trail can be followed for over twenty miles, all the way to the North Fork of the White River near the mouth of Tabor Creek. Shorter loops are available for those who are less enthusiastic about the longer hikes.

As the high ridge on the right falls away, there are some low, dark bluffs on the opposite side. Cross to the right bank at the first opportunity. There is flat valley floor on that side for two miles down to the point a wide bend takes the creek over against the west ridges. The tangle of weeds and vines in the open areas is sometimes hard to navigate from early summer through the first frosts of fall, but it is always the better side to hike.

A nice little bluff rises on the upstream side of the first valley that enters from the east, with a good pool of moderately deep water running along its base. This October I coaxed four large green sunfish into darting out of its shadows and striking a plastic worm. There weren't many bass around, but the sunfish more than made up for their absence. A higher, black-and-red-stained bluff begins along the downstream side of the tributary valley.

One beaver dam after another backs the creek into a series of deep pools for the next mile and a half. Beaver trails run up the banks and back into the woods in remarkable numbers. The hundreds of peeled limbs and dozens of felled trees give even more evidence of a thriving population of the busy rodents.

Be careful of the sharp spikes of small saplings the beaver have cut off a few inches above ground level. Recently I stepped over a log directly onto one of the pointed little stumps, and it stuck completely through my tennis shoe and into the bottom of my foot. My doctor told me that the danger of serious infection from such a wound is extreme, due in part to the type of bacteria that thrives in the soles of athletic shoes. Quick treatment and antibiotics are a must for this type of injury, or extremely dangerous infections can result.

As the creek swings at last to the west side of the valley beneath the highest ridges along the hike, you will have to walk close against high rock outcroppings that have a few shallow caves scattered along them. One deep overhang could offer safe shelter to the hiker whenever severe weather threatens. A road runs along the ridgetop and leads back to a ford across the creek at the end of the curve below. This road is a nice place to hike along and is the path I prefer because this portion of the creek is shallow and has no striking scenery. Beyond the ford the road goes on over to the northeast and intersects the portion of the Ridge Runner Trail you will be on near the end of your hike. It would shorten your trip considerably to take this road, and it is a valid option if your time is short.

If you are interested in adding a little side trip to your hike, you can take this same lane northwest to the site of the old Flat Rock School, about two miles away. A bench mark at the right-angle intersection on the flat hilltop at the school grounds indicates the altitude is 1,092 feet above sea level. The level of Noblett Creek at the ford is about 820 feet.

There is a beautiful bluff at the sharp turn below the ford and deep water running along it for about seventy-five yards. Moisture drips from its dark surface into the water below during every season of the year. I have caught many largemouth and smallmouth bass from this section over the years.

From here it is only about a half mile to Spring Creek, which is nearly nonexistent in droughts. There are many hawks along this watershed, and it is common to hear their screaming cries far above as they soar easily in the wind currents that deflect upward off the tall ridges. During the winter it is not unusual to spot bald eagles patrolling this same area.

Cross over to the west bank of the creek at the first opportunity. The left bank gets much more rugged as the slopes stretch along the prominence that divides the valleys of Noblett and Spring Creeks. There are many tall canes along the water that would make good bluegill poles if you are willing to take the time to cut some and hang them up to dry for a few weeks. Hang them with their large ends up and attach a brick or some other heavy weight to the smaller end. Some people apply a propane torch flame to the canes after they have dried, searing them just enough to make them harder and more resilient, tracing a brown spiral around the stem from one end to the other. This is a fun way to acquire a truly superior fishing pole.

Below this point you once again hike through an area of numerous beaver ponds. Watch in the thick weeds for the rear exits of their dens. Large standing trees that have been partially chewed through dot the valley floor, as well as dozens of logs from those that have already fallen. Wide beaver paths lead off from the edges of most of the ponds. Many of the dams along here will be swept away in high water, but they will be repaired and made as good as new when the stream goes back down. There is a beaver lodge a quarter of a mile above the mouth of Noblett Creek on the west side. It is in thick cover on a high mound between the main channel and a high-water channel on the far right. There are comparatively few lodges in this part of the Ozarks, the beaver seeming to prefer dens that are dug into soft dirt banks.

When the ridge falls away on the east and the valley on that side flattens out, you are only a few yards above the mouth of the creek. Cross back over to the left as soon as you can. Walk on down to Spring Creek and compare the two streams. They are about equal in water volume in the spring, but there is a marked difference during dry seasons. One recent October I found Noblett Creek to have four or five times the flow of Spring Creek. When the water is down, this portion of Spring Creek up to the Ridge Runner Trail offers little in the way of pools that hold fish.

Downstream of Noblett Creek, Spring Creek grows ever larger and deeper, offering better fishing as the depth increases. There is a low-water bridge in about a mile and a half that can also be reached by turning west off AP Highway onto a gravel road that begins three miles south of the Spring Creek bridge. This road is not numbered, but there is a sign on the left of AP indicating that the gravel road leads past a trailhead, or access point, to the Ridge Runner Trail. Turn right and drive past Horton Cemetery and the trailhead, taking the first intersection to the right a short distance from the creek. There are about ten more miles of interesting water below this point, before Spring Creek joins the North Fork. A contour map will be helpful if you would like to explore in that direction.

A makeshift table or two will usually be in evidence in the flats along either side of a faint road that leads away to the east from the mouth of Noblett Creek. It runs by a primitive campground that is primarily used by campers in hunting seasons. Spice bushes grow all over these woods, but they are especially thick to the right of the road before it begins to curve along the base of the ridge. Their leaves turn a bright yellow in fall, and along with the bright red berries that dot the stems, they make the little trees some of the most attractive in the woods.

An unusual tea can be made by boiling the tender twigs and leaves of the spice bush for about ten minutes in a covered boiler. Add sugar and perhaps a little cream, and you have a very stimulating drink. It isn't my favorite of the teas that are made from wayside plants, but some find its flavor very pleasant. No real medicinal claims are made for this tea, but it did seem to open my very clogged sinuses when I tried it, and it perked me up as much as a cup of coffee.

A spicy, almost piney smell is given off by the stems, leaves, and berries of these bushes when they are bruised. It is very hard to confuse them with another plant. I have read that the berries were dried and powdered by pioneers and used as a substitute for the cooking spices that were so hard to get during the settlement of this part of the country. Though I have yet to try cooking with them, it does sound intriguing.

Spring Creek winds in easy curves across the valley ahead and crosses the dirt road several times before you reach the trail and head up the ridges. Stay on the road but watch for the steep bluffs along your way, walking over to the creek to get a better view of any spots that catch your eye. Don't consider fishing unless the water is high enough to draw fish this far upstream.

Be exceptionally careful while hiking in the fall when thick layers of leaves cover the trails and roads. They mask rocks, limbs, and holes, making it very easy to trip and fall. Don't rush and be careful where you step. This is another time that a hiking staff proves its usefulness. When the road crosses over to the left of the creek, keep an eye along the stream for the curving line of bluffs. There is some rare deep water here, and you will see a couple of small caves right at water level that are usually used as dens by beavers. The increasingly scarce greenery that dots this part of the valley in late October is limited to clumps of alder and the hardier ferns.

After your path returns to the right bank, it parallels the water for a few yards, and then the road turns away through a thick patch of scouring rushes running toward a wide valley that opens up to the east. The pathway then divides, the right branch leading over to AP Highway about one and a half miles distant. Stay on the left fork and watch for the rock prominence that begins ahead of you to the right, well back in the trees on the other side of the tributary valley. Some shallow caves there show evidence of large flows of water coming out of them when the rains have raised the level of the groundwater. The road goes back over to the left at a beaver dam that may be in shambles early in the spring, but in good repair the next fall. It is an endless battle to keep these dams in good shape, and the beaver never give up.

As you begin to skirt the bottom of the ridge on the right, you will intersect the little lane that extends westward to the ford on Noblett Creek and on up to Flat Rock School. Proceed straight ahead and within forty yards you will see the gray, diamond-shaped Ridge Runner Trail markers on the trees to either side of the road. Turn up the branch of the trail to the left. It winds gently uphill for nearly a mile to the trailhead along County Road 293, the road to Noblett Lake. (If you go straight east on the dirt road along the creek, you come to the Spring Creek bridge on AP, about a mile and a half away.) At the trailhead take 293 to the left and finish the hike on the easy, downhill grade to Noblett Lake and the parking area below the dam. There are trails around the lake that you might want to investigate now or on a later trip.

18

SPRING CREEK ══════════

AP Highway to the Ridge Runner Trail
(Map 9, p. 124)

The bridge on AP Highway over Spring Creek is less than a mile past Howell County Road 293, the entrance to Noblett Lake. Leave your car parked beneath the large sycamore to the right of the bridge on the north bank of the creek. This comfortable little hike runs for two miles down the creek, up a part of the Ridge Runner Trail, and back down paved roads to your car. The one-way hike averages four hours for most hikers.

Immediately downstream of the bridge, the creek is shallow and runs swiftly among scattered boulders. A long, tree-covered ridge is visible to the north. There is a long, narrow hole around the first curve, with a spring dripping in over an attractive little ledge above the right bank.

The overgrown lane that leads off into the woods on the south side of the Spring Creek bridge intersects the creek below this ledge. It crosses in an open sandy area that would be a hard place to cross for even a four-wheel-drive vehicle. Below the road crossing, the creek flows straight through the middle of the valley with a one-hundred-fifty-foot ridge in sight far downstream.

An unusual beige bluff rises along the left bank, grow-

ing progressively higher and developing a slight overhang as you make your way along its base. The water
under this ledge is over waist-deep even in the middle of
the summer, and it is especially cool because of the many
small springs that feed into the stream. Beyond this bluff
there is a very deep, large pool that is exceptional for so
small a creek as this. You must skirt this pool at the base
of the steep slope to the left to avoid the dense growth
that springs up in the summer along the low bank on the
other side.

Stand quietly above this beautiful hole, or sit back unobtrusively against a log or big rock and look down into
its quiet depths for a few moments. There are more fish
and more varieties of fish here than hikers who pass hur-
riedly by can ever imagine. Some kinds that you might
see include shad, suckers, green sunfish, longear sunfish,
shadow bass, chubs, catfish, largemouth bass, smallmouth
bass, and many varieties of minnows and other smaller
species. Some of the fish in this spot are surprisingly
large. You may or may not be able to catch any of them,
but they certainly are there in good numbers.

There are spawning beds all over the lower end of this
pool that may seem to be deserted when you first walk up
to them in the summer, but if you watch patiently, you
will find that they are guarded by aggressive longear sunfish well into late June and early July. The light-colored,
conical depressions of these nests dot the bottom up and
down Spring Creek; the sunfish population seems to be
doing quite well.

Turning back to the middle of the valley as the rocky
slope tapers off below the large pool, the stream runs
along a large open field to the north. There is little deep
water in the stream beyond this point until it turns back
against another bluff on the south. A long, narrow pool
under this rock face is shaded and deep near the many
large boulders dimly visible in its depths. For several
hundred yards it runs under the branches of trees that
lean close to the rocks and make the spot seem almost
like a tunnel.

As the trees thin out farther downstream, the face of the bluff gets more and more uneven and worn. There is a small cave, some twelve to fifteen feet deep and a little less than head high, that shows signs of being used as a den. Below the cave is a double layer of ledges over the creek, the lower one barely high enough to crawl under on hands and knees.

When the bluff slants down to stream level, a wide, wooded valley appears on the left. A deer crossing runs through the bottom of the side valley and across the field to the north. If you hike through this part of Spring Creek very quietly, you will have a better than average chance of seeing a deer slipping out of the woods and moving warily across the open stream bed. Listen for any odd coughing or sneezing sounds, followed by a stomping or rattling of rocks. At certain times an aggressive or puzzled deer will react this way, trying to frighten you away or make you move in order to find out what you are.

Soon you will come to another of the overhanging bluffs that are so characteristic of this valley. The stream channel runs completely under its ten-foot-deep cornice in times of normal water flow. Tumbled boulders mark the stream past this point. The creek pushes away to the right from below the bluff and runs for a few hundred yards with only small pools along the way. There is then a straight flow beneath multiple layered ledges just before an old overgrown road crosses into an open valley that is lined with pines on its north edge.

From this point the creek is rather undistinguished for quite a distance. You will miss very little by turning away from the water at the first opportunity. The stream's channel soon divides and runs down through a long, semicircular curve. A road crosses near its lower end and leads off through the trees to the right. Follow the road to the right for about two hundred yards to its intersection with the Ridge Runner Trail. If you are interested in wild herbs, a little wandering through the woods along this part of the trail can yield rare finds. Please don't dig or pick anything you discover; some of the herbs found here (goldenseal is an exciting example) are becoming quite rare. To me the fun is in finding, identifying, and photographing rare plants, not in using them.

The trail is marked all along its course with gray, diamond-shaped signs. At a small open area with a few pines scattered on its uphill side, the trail crosses the road you are walking. There is a gray marker on a small clump of trees to the right of the road and another on a large tree to the left. The Ridge Runner Trail crosses the creek a few yards to the south and about two miles further passes the Horton Cemetery. It ends at the North Fork of the White River near CC Highway, some twenty-two miles away. The right branch leads uphill for about a mile to the Noblett Lake Trailhead on Howell County Road 293.

Turn up the trail to your right and ease your pace a little unless you are in good physical condition. The trail runs uphill for most of its course back to the trailhead, dipping down only briefly through five small ravines along the way. From the parking area at the trailhead, take 293 back to the right until you reach AP Highway. Follow AP down the steep hill to the bridge over Spring Creek and the parking spot where your car is waiting.

MAP 10

North Fork of the
White River and Indian Creek

(Chapters 19–21)

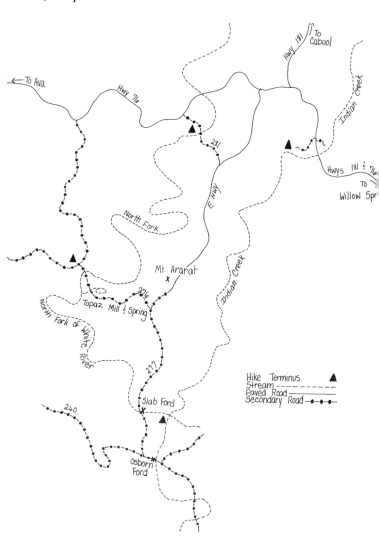

19

NORTH FORK
OF THE WHITE RIVER ══════════

Topaz Mill to Slab Ford on 277
(Map 10)

The North Fork of the White River offers two interesting one-day hikes. One of these extends from the low-water bridge at Topaz Mill to the river crossing at County Road 277. This section of the river offers sights you expect from any small stream in the Ozarks, with two bonuses: a beautiful old mill and a chance of catching rainbow trout.

The old Topaz Grist Mill lends a flavor of the past to the graceful isolation of a hike down the valley of an unspoiled stream. The mill, the old hardware store beside it, and the spring gushing from its large pool, recall a time of bustling activity when this spot seemed destined to grow into an important economic center.

The many springs that feed into the river all along its length account for its low temperature and its ability to support a healthy population of state-stocked brown and rainbow trout. The river and its tributaries have been designated a trophy trout area, where three trout of fifteen inches or more may be taken from the waters each day. If you plan to keep any of the trout you catch, make certain you have a trout stamp affixed to your fishing license.

The springs along the river vary from tiny trickles to impressive flows of over eighty million gallons a day. If you haven't seen any of the really impressive springs in the Ozarks, you might be surprised to learn that Topaz's two-million-gallon daily flow doesn't even put it in the large spring category. Nonetheless, it is the largest spring in the immediate area, and its extensive spring pool and constant flow always bring it to mind when I think of Missouri's beautiful springs.

To reach the Topaz Mill area of the North Fork, follow State Highway 181 south for ten miles from Cabool to its intersection with State Highway 76. A turn to the west for half a mile on Highway 76 brings you to E Highway. Follow E past an attractive dairy farm that boasts a classic red barn crowned with twin cupola vents and weather vanes. After going four miles you will come to the end of the asphalt, where the road runs between Mt. Ararat Cemetery and the diminutive Mt. Ararat Church with its two outhouses close by the back door.

Here, the blacktop gives way to two dirt- and rock-surfaced Douglas County roads, 277 and 276. The small, unpaved county roads are identified at intersections by small signs similar to street signs in cities. Many of these roads resemble private drives and lanes, often passing close between farmhouses and outbuildings, making you wonder if you have made a wrong turn and wound up somewhere you shouldn't be. Those who decide to turn down these small roads and go exploring find that sometimes they actually do dead-end on private property without any warning. This can involve embarrassing moments turning around in someone's front yard. It is best to stick to the roads suggested in this guide or to obtain detailed maps of the area, such as those from the Missouri Department of Natural Resources.

County Road 277 turns to the left as the asphalt ends and intercepts the North Fork at Slab Ford, a concrete structure without culverts that the river has to flow over in an attractive man-made waterfall. This ford makes a good point to end a hike of about five miles from Topaz Mill.

To reach the mill and the upper end of this hike, continue straight on 276 down the gradual slope into the
valley of the White River. The river valley here is about
two hundred feet below the general level of the surrounding hills. Areas of pasture and woodland alternate all
along the stream. When you reach the floor of the valley,
the road parallels the river for a few hundred yards as it
passes through a private farm. To the left of the road as
you approach the river, you will see a new metal storage
building, an old general store, and the well-preserved
Topaz Mill. The mill and store are in private hands and
closed to the public. Neither dates back to the original
settlers, the present mill being built in 1895 and the general store in 1913. The first mill, of which no obvious
trace remains, was built across the road from the present
one in about 1840.

Topaz Spring sends its clear water flowing from across
the road under a small bridge and past the mill. The
rockwork that formerly carried the spring water to the
new mill building has recently been refurbished and is in
excellent condition. The road swings left beyond the spring
and crosses the river on a narrow low-water bridge of
concrete under which the river normally flows through
three large openings. In high water, the river rushes over
this bridge and it is impassable.

Across the river, the road you are traveling ends at
another county road, which runs north and south along
this part of the stream. Turn left for a few yards until you
cross a shallow spring branch that flows directly across
the road. Beyond the little stream there is a small turnoff
to the right with just enough room for one or two vehicles
to park. Pull in here and get your gear together.

You should lock your car or truck, but things are seldom tampered with in this part of the Ozarks. It is hard
for those from other areas to believe, but local people
hardly ever lock their cars and many don't even own a
key to their house. The easiest access to the river from
your parking spot is down the spring branch you just
crossed. Wade down the little stream to its mouth. There

is a faint trail opposite the parking area, but it is infre-
quently traveled and more difficult to make your way
along because of the thick undergrowth and its steep
slope as it nears the water. This part of the North Fork is
narrow and swift, with deep water only around an occasional fallen tree. About a hundred yards downstream,
the branch from Topaz Spring enters from the left, greatly
increasing the volume of the river's flow and noticeably
dropping the water temperature.

Under the overhanging branches on the right bank below the spring, the water is shaded and a little deeper. I
have caught quite a few nice smallmouth here, and one
July I was lucky enough to take a twenty-two-inch rainbow trout from the shaded run beneath the trees. Trout
are much more common farther down the river, but once
in a while they are found far up the headwaters and in
the smaller feeder streams.

The river now flows over large slabs of exposed limestone for a short distance as the woods on the right give
way to dairy pasture. These fields border the west side of
the river for the next three-quarters of a mile. The left
bank is still heavily wooded and is littered with large
boulders that extend out into deep, still water. One hole,
above a ford where cattle cross the river, is especially
large and deep and is a good spot to fish lures or live bait
slowly and patiently across the bottom.

As the water becomes shallower and narrower, the woods
on the left are also replaced by pasture, and you are at the
beginning of the huge curve of a long, entrenched meander. You could cut straight across the bend to save nearly
a mile of hiking if you are in a hurry. If you do, however,
you will miss two or three beautiful, deep holes beneath
the steep, tree-covered slopes that lie along the outside of
the large curve.

If you hike this region in summer or early fall, keep an
eye out for the wild impatiens (spotted touch-me-not, or
jewelweed). The plants grow to five feet on weak, watery
stems and are covered with cornucopia-shaped orange
flowers. The leaves are soft blue-green and egg-shaped.

The alternate name touch-me-not comes from the plants' explosive expulsion of their seeds if they are touched when the pods are dry and ready to release them.

The leaves of this plant, when crushed and applied to poison ivy blisters, make one of the best remedies for the rash I have ever seen. The speed with which the leaves begin to relieve the inflammation varies from person to person, but I have never seen the remedy fail. Every summer I collect several leaves, removing only a few leaves from a particular stem so as to avoid lasting damage to the plants. I puree them in a blender with methyl alcohol and store the solution extracted from them in the refrigerator. This becomes the poison ivy cure for my family and any of my students who fall victim to the rash.

Once you are around the meander, the stream flows southeasterly, bearing back to the south for nearly a mile through heavily forested land. There is an occasional deep spot scoured out against one bank or the other in this stretch of the river, but for the most part the water is shallow. Although beavers are common on this part of the North Fork, they are seldom seen except near sunrise or sunset. During the daylight hours they hole up in dens they have dug in the softer banks. Don't look for any beaver dams on the main river; on streams with enough deep water, dams aren't necessary for the beavers' needs. Most of the smaller streams flowing into the river are broadened and deepened by beaver dams and side trips along these attractive little creeks are usually a lot of fun.

If you are walking on the bank near the river, watch for the numerous holes that are the rear exits of underground beaver dens. They are connected to the stream by horizontal tunnels. Stepping into one of these holes could result in an injury that might make it hard for you to get back to your car without help. It is interesting to find the occasional slides worn into the steeper mud banks where beavers habitually skid down to the water, often dragging freshly cut limbs with them. If you are lucky enough to see these slides in use, take time to watch and snap a few photographs.

The faint tracks of roads parallel the river on both sides here, running back into the trees several yards away from the water. I like to walk along these whenever I get tired of wading, searching for seasonal plants and blooms and hoping to catch sight of some of the area's abundant wildlife. If you hike one of these roads very quietly and are lucky, you might see a flock of wild turkeys or some of the numerous deer.

One early March day I was walking the north road and ran across the largest flock of wild turkeys I can remember seeing. The toms were strutting and displaying their impressive tail feathers, and it seemed as though the entire forest floor ahead of me moved when they became aware of my approach. The prospect of similar experiences keeps me hiking Ozark streams year after year.

There are two small watercress springs along the river in the next few hundred yards, before you get to the next bend. One lies back from the north bank and one close by the south. The spring on the left originates fifty yards back in the trees and wanders to the river along a small channel. The one on the right flows out from the edge of a bar near the river, and its flow sinks into the gravel before it actually reaches the main stream. Many people enjoy the sharp taste of watercress in salads, but possible pollution of the water discourages sampling the cress from these springs.

When the river swings around to flow straight south, there is an overgrown road back in the woods on the west bank all the way down to the mouth of Clifty Creek. I have surprised woodcock in this moist woodland several times. It might be more truthful to say that we surprised each other, because the sudden, darting appearance of this robin-sized bird immediately underfoot is enough to make calmer hearts than mine skip a beat. Woodcock are easy to recognize by their elongated bill, rust-colored tail feathers, and halting, twisting flight as they dodge away through the trees. Woodcock and robins both feed on worms, but robins are brave enough to make your lawn their dinner table, while woodcock are nocturnal, solitary, and shy, feeding in the damp soil of shaded woods. Since woodcock are not especially common, it is a treat to see one.

Clifty Creek enters the North Fork from the west on a sharp bend as the river turns again to the east. If you have the time, consider taking a side trip up the pretty Clifty Creek valley. The river here is bordered by a large meadow and steep, wooded ridges that bend the flow gradually in a half-mile curve to the northeast. The water is deep and shaded along the steep ridge bank, where big smallmouth and goggle-eye often lurk in the shadows.

At the end of the meadow, the bank on that side rises abruptly to an impressive vertical cliff of a hundred fifty feet. A short distance downstream this rock face intersects another even higher ridge at right angles. The taller bluff has a house on top that presents one of the most marvelous views in the entire region from its back deck.

The east-west bluff drops away at its far end into a deep, narrow valley. It is drained by an intermittent spring branch that enters from the north into a pool where the river makes a ninety-degree turn to the right. The pool is floored with a light-tinted layer of limestone that shows off the color of the river's deep, clear, mineral-laden water in an astounding green when conditions are just right. Spots like this are beautiful in any season, but bright, clear days in late winter, when the river is at its clearest after a prolonged dry spell, seem to bring out colors in the water that can be seen at no other time of the year. This bend in the river is a wonderful place to sit back on a handy log and relax in the sunshine while enjoying the scenery.

Several times I have had a pair of wood ducks lead me a merry chase up and down this part of the stream as I tried to get a closer look at them. Don't be surprised if you see one of these ducks perched on a limb high over the water. They are tree ducks and nest in hollow trees or special boxes that are put out in some areas for them. This trait and their shrill, whistling cry make them easy to identify.

The river now flows straight and narrow to the south

between the cliff and a wide meadow on the west. The last time I waded the North Fork, I saw two ospreys spiraling out from above the ridges and over this open field. White underneath, with a conspicuous crook at the end of their wings, their black "wrist" markings make these uncommon fish hawks easy to identify. The ospreys were a rare sight and not something you should expect to see, but keep an eye to the sky here and along the entire river for hawks and the not-so-uncommon eagles.

You should learn to identify turkey vultures to keep from confusing them with eagles. The black vulture is far more common than the eagle, with a much shorter head, narrower tail, and wings that are tipped up in a distinctive dihedral V as it flies. Until you gain a little experience you may have to consult a bird identification book to help you, but soon you will find that distinguishing the two is not difficult.

At the southern end of this run, the river swings once more to the east at another sharp corner. A small spring enters from the right into a deep, blue-green hole that is larger than the last big pool upstream and almost its equal in color. Beyond this point there is a long, wide stretch of river that is much like a small lake nearly a fourth of a mile long. The water is stilled and deepened by the concrete ford on County Road 277. Live bait, such as minnows and crayfish, fished on the bottom through this pool can pay off in catches of bass, sunfish, and catfish. Slowly fished artificial lures might also work, but I have had little luck with them here.

There is a large dairy pasture on the left with a barn at the top of the hill. This pasture goes all the way to 277. If you want to walk through this pasture, ask permission before you begin your trip down from Topaz Hill. The farm has changed owners over the years, but I have never had any problem obtaining permission to cross once the owners realize I am not a hunter. Some landowners along the river post signs denying you the right to do anything on their property, so stick within the banks of the river if you are not sure of the situation.

You can end your hike at 277 if you wish, or if you are still feeling spry, continue on for another mile to a low-water bridge on County Road 260 at a point called Osborn Ford. This ford is a half mile left from the dead end of 277 into 260. Osborn Ford bridge is another ideal point to end the hike and could also be the starting point for another hike farther down the river. Park on the right just before you reach the bridge.

If you continue downriver from 277, you will see a high ridge about three-tenths of a mile immediately ahead. This is the divide between the North Fork watershed and that of Indian Creek, a stream described in chapter 21. The rocks at the top of the ridge are stained black by a coating of minerals leached from the ground. The cap-rock of the river is a resistant layer that has stood up to the weathering effects of time, while the underlying rocks are softer and less resistant. They wear away slowly and undermine the top layers.

At the end of the divide you can see that the very end of the ridge has been so undercut that it has broken off. A large fragment is embedded in the slope below. Seeing this fallen rock always makes me uneasy over the number of times I have stood on the edge of a high, projecting ledge to enjoy some spectacular view.

The North Fork sweeps back to the right along the promontory at its junction with Indian Creek and runs past a jumble of large rocks into a beautiful, deep hole a short distance downstream. A long rope hanging above the water of this pool gives evidence that this is a local swimming hole. Continuing around a couple of gentle curves that have some moderately deep water on their outer banks, the river straightens out and flows under the low-water bridge at Osborn Ford. This should mark the end of your one-day, extended hike down the North Fork of the White River.

If you are interested in continuing downriver, Osborn Ford could be the beginning of another hike, which continues for two and a half miles to another low-water bridge at Hale Ford and for a mile and a half beyond that to the bridge and campground at Hebron access; however, the river gets increasingly deeper and wider as you go through this section. This makes the possibility of catching larger fish more likely, but the deeper waters and more overgrown banks make fishing and wading this part of the river much more difficult. I hiked this lower section years ago, but not recently enough to give an accurate description of the region. If you are in the area, and are so inclined, you might consider extending your hike farther downstream.

Hop hornbeam hanging out over the South Prong of Jacks Fork below the bridge on Highway 137 north of Willow Springs.

Six baby wood ducks paddling frantically upstream on the South Prong of Jacks Fork. The mother hen was hiding nearby.

Attractive patterns in sheets of limestone lining the bed of Little Pine Creek.

View from the ridge over Big Pine Creek.

Gaudy—and toxic—jack-o'-lantern mushroom (omphalotus oleanius) along Big Pine Creek.

Maidenhair ferns covering the face of a small bluff at Stillhouse Hollow.

Purple coneflowers at Stillhouse Hollow.

Spring branch entering Noblett Creek at the campground below Noblett Lake Dam.

Beaver dam on Noblett Creek above its intersection with Spring Creek.

Upper Spring Creek above Carman Spring.

A patch of goldenseal growing near the Ridgerunner Trail below Noblett Lake.

Topaz Mill and general store on the North Fork.

Topaz Mill spring on the North Fork of the White River.

The flume at Dawt Mill along the North Fork.

20

WHITE RIVER ========

Upstream from Topaz Mill
(Map 10, p. 154)

        Instead of turning left after you cross the river beyond Topaz Mill as you would for the hike downstream (described in the last chapter), turn to the right and drive up past a beautiful swimming hole with large gravel bars along its lower margin. You could park here on the bars, but there is a better place a little upstream where a short drive loops through a camping area on the right, between the main road and the river. This is private land, but it is available for public parking. A sign warns that the area is closed from eight-thirty at night until eight in the morning.

  Another car could be left at the low-water bridge on Douglas County 281, which intersects Highway 76 less than a quarter of a mile west of the highway bridge over the river. The best parking spots are to the west of the low-water bridge; the spots to the east are in deep, rather loose gravel beds. Since 281 goes on across the river to intersect E Highway north of Mount Ararat Church, you could come in from that direction if you wish.

  For several years I had fished the North Fork below Topaz Mill, but I never really considered going upstream until recently. The river is extremely small at the mill and above the county road crossing. It is even smaller far upstream at Highway 76. Logic told me that there would not be enough deep water through this section to make a hike worthwhile; logic served me about as well this time as it usually does. There is actually *more* deep water in the six miles above the mill than in the first six miles below it. Some of the holes upstream are far bigger and deeper than anything you would expect to find on so little a river.

There is some moderate water down the steep slope beside the campground parking area that is waist-deep even in a dry September. Flat sheets of limestone line the bottom in fissured layers. The river then runs seventy-five yards through shallows along the field to the right, the same field that contains Topaz Mill Spring.

Past this stretch the water deepens against the left bank, where large rocks have slid down the slope into the stream. The ledge on the left develops into an overhang that sticks out four or five feet from the bank, with pockets of deep water beneath it all the way up to the sharp bend ahead. A very wide, long field stretches above the bank to the north. I have caught many longear sunfish and goggle-eye in this section, but never any bass.

There is a deep, circular pool around the curve which has been full of stubborn cows that prevented my catching anything each time I have been there. Swift water runs through a series of rapids that splash over pretty ledges above the pool. The little ledges stair-step up the river, one after the other, for about fifty yards.

Wood mint grows everywhere along the river, on the bars, and in the woods along the banks. Its dark-green, fuzzy leaves have a quilted texture with deeply etched veins. The stems are square, as in all members of the mint family. Long flower stalks crown the top of the plants and open into series of tiny blue flowers. The delightful smell of crushed mint follows you everywhere when you walk through overgrown sections of the bank in the fall. Rub the leaves between your fingers to establish which plant is the mint if you are in doubt. You can make a pleasant tea from fresh or dried leaves.

Above the series of ledges, a spring flows in from close against the left bank. I noticed it the first time, as I have many other springs, by feeling the extra chill it added to the water before I ever saw the spring itself.

In the wide, shallow holes upstream, there are usually more fish than one would think. Even if you don't see fish, cast out and let your lure lie still for a while on the bottom. I have caught dozens of fish here, representing some six different species.

A little road cuts through the slope to the right and crosses the river through shallow rapids below a wide pool. The last time I fished this pool, I waited for two considerate cows to wade slowly out of the water and then caught four smallmouth in quick succession before the silt from their passing had even settled. It seems these fish have gotten used to the cows wading around in the river and aren't spooked by them.

The long field continues on the left and a pretty hillside rises on the right. The dirt bank on that side goes up and levels off on a crown of rock topped by a little ledge that is a good spot to climb up and walk along. The river grows shallow as it winds gently back and forth ahead of you. Its overall course for the next mile is through a huge oxbow bend to the left.

A few trees were beginning to turn bright colors when I was here one mid-September day, and leaves were drifting down to the water in surprising numbers. The yellows of soft maples, sycamore, spice bushes, and hackberries were everywhere, but the most attractive coloration belonged to the sassafras, with its unusual mix of orange and green. Nowhere can you enjoy the autumn more than along an Ozark stream.

The little stream that enters on the right, as the river angles to the left, comes from a spring beneath a dirt bank only a few yards back into the woods. A large, dry valley comes in farther up on that same side at a spot where there is some deep water near a cattle crossing. On my last hike here I was up on that bank watching a groundhog scurrying along through the weeds when a gust of wind accompanied by an incredible racket scared me out of my wits. The breeze rudely shook the dry bean pods of the coffee trees that grow here in large numbers and their frenzied rattling made a louder noise than I would have ever thought possible. I don't know what I thought it was at first, but I certainly didn't think trees were responsible; a person's blood pressure should be immune to attack by trees. A coffee tree looks something like a honey locust tree that has lost its thorns, and the dried seeds have been roasted and used as a passable substitute for coffee.

A short distance away, rock ledges emerge from ten- to twelve-foot bluffs, the little overhangs leading upstream above a hole that is bordered on both sides by open areas. The ridge on the right becomes steeper until it stands more than eighty feet over the floor of the valley. Above a series of rocks that dot the channel, the river angles more to the left and a spring branch enters on the outside of the curve. I have never followed it back to its source because of the extreme amount of undergrowth that lines it most of the year.

As the river leaves the ridges, the woods close in thickly on both sides and the stream opens up into a giant pool that stretches for over one hundred fifty yards ahead. One recent September day I caught enough smallmouth in this pool, some of them fourteen inches in length, to take home a limit of keepers if I had wanted to do so.

You will have to get out of the water to get around this hole because it is too deep to wade, even at the very edges. The bank on the right is a more level walking surface than the other side, but it is also more overgrown. Well beyond the steep slope on the left is an open field if you want to go up that far for some easier hiking. The upper end of the pool suddenly becomes shallow at a series of flat ledges. Up ahead you will see the best bluffs you have walked along so far, and it is necessary to cross over to the opposite bank to get around them.

Wading this river—or any other stream, pond, or swamp in backwater areas—will cause large bubbles to rise from decaying vegetation that has collected on the bottom. These bubbles are created by methane (natural gas), which will burn if you hold a blazing stick over the water while stirring the leaves with your wading staff. The flame is so clear that it is best seen near dark. More than a few times these methane bubbles have been used by confidence men to convince the unwary that a piece of property has natural gas and oil deposits beneath it, but this phenomenon has nothing to do with subsurface riches. The decay of plant or animal matter where no oxygen can reach it will produce methane, and a pile of leaves on the bottom of a still pool is an ideal place for it to form.

Below the hollowed-out lower surface of the next bluff, I have caught several smallmouth of keeping size. This spot is nowhere near as big and deep as many others along the river, and catching fish here always reminds me that I have caught more fish in smaller holes and pockets than I have in the really big pools. Don't take an inordinate time to fish deeper areas: cast every few feet as you wade slowly upstream and then move on without going over the pool again.

The river now runs to the left at another pool that has rocks sloping into the water from the right. A slough goes off the creek on that side, and the bank gets too steep to walk along. The first swift riffles in over a half mile of the river tumble down from around the little bend ahead. The channel winds gently back and forth until a field closes in on the right, and a road crosses from that field toward another pasture that is out of sight behind the trees of the opposite bank.

The river now becomes much more intimate and shaded, its bank held closely among thick woods on both sides. There are no fields visible, but they are there, hidden behind the screening trees. This area is enchanting, even though there are no cliffs or spectacular rock formations in sight. In a few yards, as the channel runs along a gently sloping ridge on the left, you will come to a long, beautiful hole that is the largest from Slab Ford to Highway 76. Halfway up the pool is a deep, overhanging ledge that starts about eight feet over the water with a crown of rock above it that is ten to twelve feet thick. I have caught several big bass near this ledge.

A short distance upstream the pool gets so deep that you have to get out on the right bank to go on upriver. As you walk up the bank, go back over to the pool often to cast in any spot that is open enough to give you room. This hole ends in a shallow area that gives way to lively, splashing rapids extending upstream for over a hundred yards.

The third of the deepest holes on the upper river begins above these rapids and moves to the right toward a giant, square-edged boulder sitting in the stream with one of its corners angled toward you as you wade upstream. This large block of limestone has very deep water around its base, and I have seen largemouth bass up to three pounds darting into its shadows. Largemouth are easily distinguished from smallmouth because of their green coloration and the distinctive dark line running down the sides.

There is a right-angle bend beyond this boulder that runs along a well-kept, grassy area bordering a house and several outbuildings. A large field opens up to the left beyond the house, and quite often there are cows in this part of the river. Another field runs high up beyond the right bank with a little road on its upper margin that can take you back downriver to your starting point should you want to cut your hike short.

The river winds through another mile-long oxbow, swinging far around to the left ahead of you. Honey locust trees grow all over the bar across from the high bluffs that line the outside of the big curve. The larger trees have frightening clusters of giant thorns sticking out four to six inches from their trunks. Honey locust branches are covered with large, beanlike pods filled with a pulp that is sweet and edible when ripe. The pods look very much like those of the coffee tree—but they don't rattle so rudely in a strong breeze.

Immediately below the next swift riffle, pretty ledges

project two to three feet over the water at a thirty-foot-long hole that is usually full of fish. Every time I have caught a fish here, it was followed in by two or three even larger fish. There has to be a corollary to Murphy's Law involved in this somehow.

The curve of one river sharpens to the left and the cliffs above you rise well beyond a hundred feet. There are occasional deep pockets on this bend until the water shallows into narrow runs and a field appears on the right. After the channel divides, a road crosses below a bluff that springs up along a ridge to the left. A long hole running along its base is often filled with a thick growth of yellow-green algae. The water here is moderately deep, but the algae makes it look even deeper than it really is.

The river now turns sharply along beautiful ledges and over wide sheets of limestone. The stream bends back upon itself and curves around the other side of the ridge that has been paralleling the river on the right. There are a few buildings high up on the outside of the sharpest part of the curve. Farther upstream a moderate hole floored with more limestone sheets interrupts the long run toward the next ridge.

The stream has now emerged into open fields and bars with few trees along its banks. There is a big, marshy spring to the right along the low ridge that closes slowly in well ahead of you. In a few hundred yards a fence runs into the river from the left at a deep hole where the ridge finally intrudes against the right bank. An overgrown road angles up the slope on the far edge of this pool. Beyond the fence the river turns hard to the left at a large, nearly rectangular hole.

The cliff is a vertical wall here but quickly drops away, and the valley becomes wide and flat on both sides of the stream. A road crosses the river and leads to sheds and barns a quarter of a mile away on the right. After a long, sweeping turn to the east that has a few small pools and narrow runs along its course, you will arrive at the low-water bridge on Douglas County Road 281.

If you are walking back downstream, watch for the

road that angles up the lowering ridge on the left side after you cross back over the fence below the rectangular hole. Follow it up and over the ridge to cut off the oxbow. As you drop down the far side, pick up the road you passed earlier that runs around the end of the ridge you see on the other side of the valley. Follow it down into the next pasture and cut off the next big curve, going back to the river before you get too close to the buildings at its lower end.

Watch for the field starting on the left side of the river before you get to the ninety-degree turn of the channel. The road I mentioned earlier runs along the upper edge of the overgrown pasture. It leads down the valley, across a concrete cattle gap, and back into the woods. Turn right at the first intersection past the cattle gap. This takes you across the creek and into the extremely long pasture that arcs for about a mile to the county road where you parked. These shortcuts will enable you to walk back in less than a third the time it took you to hike upstream along the river channel.

21

INDIAN CREEK ═══════════════════

*Slab Ford on County Road 277 to
Highway 76
(Map 10, p. 154)*

Indian Creek is an impressive tributary of the
North Fork of the White River that has a constant flow of
water even in the driest seasons. Long stretches of beautiful, rushing rapids and shallow rills are interrupted by
occasional pools of dark green water that are second to
none in the Ozarks. In the central and lower parts of the
section described in this chapter, there are impressive
bluffs, ledges, and spring tributaries—enough to satisfy
any hiker. In times of drought a portion of the stream has
been known to go underground for up to half a mile, only
to reappear with its current undiminished farther downstream. At times, fishing on Indian Creek can be spectacular, and even on the least productive trips I have
managed to land at least a limit of keeper smallmouth.

The upper terminus of the hike can be reached by taking Highway 76 west from the caution light on Highway
60 at Willow Springs, past the intersection with Highway
181, to the bridge over the creek eight miles west. The
most convenient parking is in the large area to the north
of the bridge, but those not afraid of difficult roads can
take the rough track that begins past the bridge on the

south and intersects the creek some three-quarters of a mile below. This road is narrow and I have gotten stuck along it before, but it does bypass a long stretch of shallow, unimpressive water. If you drive all the way down to the creek, the parking spot is at a small turnaround on the left a short distance before you reach the stream.

If you are coming to the area from the west, this spot is most easily approached by turning south off Highway 60 onto Highway 181 at Cabool. Follow 181 for ten miles until it joins 76, where you should turn back to the east for three miles to the Indian Creek bridge. There is a scenic overlook that stands high above the upper valley of Indian Creek at the start of the steep grade down to the creek. This part of the stream is attractive from high above because of the steep ridges and deep valleys, but the view for the hiker at water level is better farther downstream.

The parking area at the lower end of this hike is on the North Fork of the White River a few hundred yards from the mouth of Indian Creek. To reach it, go west on Highway 76 to the point Highway 181 turns off to Cabool. A half mile west of 181, turn south on E Highway and follow it past the large barn on the right to the end of the pavement at Mount Ararat Church. A short distance down the gravel road, turn left on County Road 277 between the house and barns of a dairy farm. Follow this little road to its crossing of the North Fork at Slab Ford.

The parking area is to the left of the road on the far side of the concrete slab. There is a dirt road that turns left past the parking area and goes down to the river below the junction of Indian Creek. It is often full of mudholes and deep ruts. Don't go down to the river this way unless you have a vehicle with high ground clearance, perhaps even one with four-wheel drive.

This trip is an exceptionally long one for a two-way hike, taking a good five hours of steady walking to make it in one direction. The five-hour estimate allows little time for fishing and sight-seeing. If you do plan to retrace your steps, you should limit your trip to the most scenic sections, which are at the downstream end. The best fishing is usually in this portion of the creek also. I will describe the hike up from Slab Ford and indicate the spot where I usually stop my trek upstream and fish my way back down.

Immediately downstream from the ford on the North Fork there is a small spring branch that comes in from the left at the first curve. If it is not too overgrown, take the time to walk up to the spring that rises against the bluff across the field to the north. In late summer go up the branch a few yards to see the blossoms of the rare yellow-flowered variety of wild impatiens (touch-me-not, or jewelweed). The leaves of this plant make an effective home remedy for poison ivy, which I have used with some frequency. (A more detailed description of the remedy and its preparation is given in chapter 19.)

There is usually good, fishable water at the beginning and at the end of this first curve below Slab Ford. A short distance beyond, the river runs straight along the prominence that separates the watersheds of the North Fork and Indian Creek. The ridge is narrow and ends in a pretty ledge of black rock, part of which has broken off and tumbled down the very tip of the prominence. Until the leaves have fallen from the trees, this tumbled rock is very hard to see.

As a bluff comes into view ahead of you on the North Fork, Indian Creek enters from the left. It is obvious that the amount of water coming down the creek is considerably less than that in the river, but it is an important tributary. Indian Creek is very shallow and swift with little deep water for a long distance above its confluence with the North Fork. Don't be impatient or disappointed at the lower portion of the creek; there are many beautiful areas farther upstream.

The first big curve on the stream turns to the right, and as it does, the ridge on the left grows higher, displaying a rock face high above you. A small road crosses the creek around this bend, and there is some deep water above the road with an attractive wooded ridge ahead. The road leads back to the right through woods and pastures, eventually intersecting the North Fork well below the mouth of Indian Creek. To the left it cuts off across a large bend and avoids much difficult walking through the streambed. If you are interested in making better time while going upstream, follow the road across the bar. You can stay on this road for a mile or more across a large field, through some dense woods, and past a smaller field, before returning to the river in another thick stand of trees.

If you take the road, you will notice a small spur that goes over to the creek in the middle of the first patch of woods. This leads to one of the longest and deepest holes of beautiful green water on the entire stream. There is little to be gained by hiking up the creek instead of the road. All the deep water in this vicinity is near the open hole at the end of the little spur.

The main branch of this road comes back to the creek below a shallow run that has an open field above the bank on the right. The stream is not impressive here, but I have consistently caught fish in this area, including a very nice smallmouth my last trip up. You should carefully fish any spots that are waist-deep or deeper, no matter how clear they are, especially if they are shaded or if the current is broken by large rocks, logs, or ledges that offer any kind of shelter for fish.

Above this point the creek bends around to the right at a muddy slough, quickly turns back left, and then runs straight and narrow for a hundred yards. After another little turn there are some areas of deep water along a rock face with layers that tilt at an angle of about twenty degrees as they enter the water. There are several large rocks in the depths beneath the bluff and even deeper water past the spot the last rock layer enters the water.

The creek turns sharply to the right beyond this ledge, and a small alternate channel hugs the left bank where a little spring adds its water to the main flow. To the left of the next long, straight stretch, there is a wide, overgrown bar parallel to the creek. You can walk through here to avoid harder hiking down along the water.

Above this bar is a wide pasture beyond a narrow stand

of trees. At the end of the bar the creek makes a ninety-degree turn to the left and winds easily back and forth for several hundred yards. There are now small pockets of deep water along a twenty- to twenty-five-foot dirt bank on the left. A large field is on the right, and fences and corrals are visible in the distance. A road through this field crosses the creek at a shallow ford and leads up to a house and barn that sit back from the creek on the left. Stay in the creek bed or gravel bars here and in any areas in which you might cause offense by walking across private property.

There is a broad gravel bar that extends back to the edge of the woods above the house, and the stream skirts the upper end of the bar, straightening out along a lovely overhanging bluff. The bluff is small, with an overhang some ten feet high and eight feet deep, but its beauty is magnified by masses of maidenhair ferns. Water drips softly in its damp recesses even in late summer. The fact that I invariably catch a smallmouth or two from the pool above the bluff makes it even more attractive. There are low rock ledges at water level upstream from the bluff on the other side of the creek, and the same field that was opposite the house downstream continues up above that bank behind a thin line of trees.

From this spot Indian Creek turns to the right into a chaotic area of large rocks that have tumbled into the water from an overhanging ledge. Very deep water surrounds the debris from the ledge and I have caught numbers of large fish from the depths around the boulders on all of my hikes. In a few yards you will come to an even deeper overhang. It is set back a little uphill from the water and offers a safe, snug shelter during threatening weather.

A high ridge begins above the right bank and grows gradually taller as you go upstream. The ridge angles off through the woods along a small, spring-fed tributary as the main stream arcs to the left. There is a deep pool at the mouth of the little spring branch. If you are interested in a little additional diversion and have the time, you should walk up this feeder stream. It flows by several interesting rock formations, and soon another creek channel enters it from the left. This second creek sends waterfalls six to ten feet in height over at least three ledges when there is enough rainfall.

The impressive bluff line above the next curve on Indian Creek has two rock faces exposed: one is near water level and the other is eighty to a hundred feet higher. The creek then gets quite deep before it takes a big swing to the left away from the bluff and toward high rock ledges on the opposite side. Two large slabs of rock have fallen from those ledges into the stream, and the larger, downstream mass exhibits a sharply pointed face that resembles the prow of a ship sticking out of the water.

Around the next bend is another overhanging ledge with a fallen section that is standing up vertically in the water. The topmost edge of this collapsed portion leans against the lip of the ledge, where it must have toppled back for support after splashing into the creek. Though not really a cave, there is a roomy shelter behind this big slab of limestone. All of the larger rocks in this part of the stream have deep pools of clear, green water around them.

After a quick swing to the right, the creek is flowing through a shallow run with open pasture to the right and a low, wooded bank on the left. An ATV road crosses a ford at the end of this run. Upstream a long bend turns sharply along a wooded ridge. To the left a farmhouse and some barns sit well back from the stream across a steeply sloping field. You can walk up the road to the right of the ford and climb a short distance up the ridge to an overlook for a good view of this portion of the creek's watershed. Please don't go beyond the private property sign on the gate that blocks the road farther up the ridge.

If you plan to retrace your steps and fish your way back down, this is a good place to stop. There are a few nice pools upstream of this point, but the best scenery and fishing are back downstream. It takes two more hours of fast walking—much longer if you do some fishing and hike slowly—to go upstream from here to the Highway 76 bridge over Indian Creek. There is a swift run of rapids around the next bend to the left, followed by intermittent holes of deep water along the ridge to the west. Look far up the slope of the ridge for the rock outcroppings high above you. This area is much more striking in late fall and winter when the leaves don't block your view.

At the next very sharp curve to the right, the creek leaves the ridge on the left and flows straight for about a quarter of a mile, parallel to another equally high ridge on the south. There is a high dirt cutbank on the north side at the beginning of the run with moderately deep water that is usually good for one or two big fish. A large, grassy meadow opens out beyond this dirt bank, with a farmhouse visible on its far edge.

At the end of this straight stretch is a small spring branch flowing in at the beginning of a long curve that takes the main creek around to the north. In dry years Indian Creek goes underground above this bend, and you could be walking up a dry creek bed for up to half a mile. Upstream is a wide area of gravel bars through which the creek winds until it straightens out against a field on the right. The next run leads up to a long, wide pool that sometimes supports a large population of bass and goggle-eye.

The last time I waded this section, the largest beaver I have ever seen quietly slid off the east bank and swam right toward me as I waded the long pool. He gave me quite a start, but it turned out that I was between the beaver and its den and he didn't have any hostile intentions at all. He slowly disappeared downstream into a tunnel in the dirt bank while my heart tried to work its way down from my throat and slow down to its normal rate. I have mentally kicked myself over and over for not getting a picture of this beaver, but I don't think too well when I'm scared silly.

The next half mile upstream is always hard to describe accurately because of constantly shifting pools and shallow riffles. There are long, swift rapids with an occasional pocket of deep water, but the exact positions change from season to season. Eventually you will come to a long pool with several big rocks along the left side; it has yielded some of the finest fish I have caught in Indian Creek.

The valley soon narrows and the creek becomes a little swifter. There are no real bluffs, but the ridges are steep and close to the water on both sides. A few small caves can be seen. The good fishing spots here will be on the left side of the creek in grassy pools and around scattered boulders.

At a slight curve to the right, below the prettiest rapids in several miles, a small dirt road crosses the stream diagonally up to the left. This road leads back to Highway 76 in three-quarters of a mile and bypasses a section of the creek in which there is little deep water or memorable scenery. There are some spots along its length where a vehicle could be parked, as mentioned at the start of this chapter, or you can go all the way back up to the parking area beyond the bridge. The creek continues above the bridge for several miles, growing progressively smaller. The valley gets narrower and deeper, but offers little interesting scenery to anyone walking at creek level. There is nothing above here to compare to the spots you have seen downstream.

MAP 11

Fox Creek

(Chapter 22)

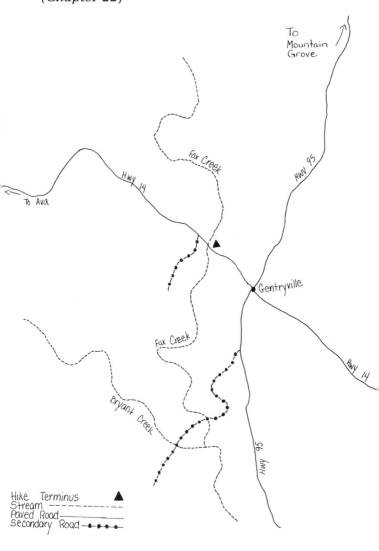

To Mountain Grove

Fox Creek

Hwy 14

Hwy 95

To Ava

Fox Creek

Gentryville

Hwy 14

Bryant Creek

Hwy 95

Hike Terminus ▲
Stream - - - - - -
Paved Road ————
Secondary Road •••••

22

FOX CREEK ═══════════════════════

(Map 11)

       Fox Creek is a small tributary of Bryant Creek that can be easily reached by taking Highway 95 south of Mountain Grove for twenty-one miles to its intersection with Highway 14 at Gentryville. Follow Highway 14 to the bridge over Fox Creek at the bottom of the first valley to the west. The only parking area is parallel to the highway on the northeast side of the bridge. There are no spots to park down the dirt road that leads south after you cross over the creek. This road leads only to private homes and farms.

  Fox Creek has a moderate but consistent flow throughout the dry summer months. It runs past Highway 14 in a shallow, relatively straight run for close to half a mile. Several electric lines pass overhead to houses along the stream, and there is one area of limestone ledges and attractive little rapids just beyond the first set of wires. The only heights are low ridges to the east that are broken by occasional tributary valleys. In its first real bend, the creek veers slightly left along a twelve- to fifteen-foot bluff at the end of a ridge, but there is seldom any deep water here.

  Soon a barbed wire fence crosses the stream in a long, unsupported span. A house is visible back in the field to the right. What looks like a small road crosses the water below the fence, but it deteriorates to rutted cattle trails in the field to the east.

Kingfishers are unusually prevalent on this part of Fox Creek. Look for these large, blue, and white birds sitting on dead snags overlooking the creek as they search the water below for small fish. Their unusual call, which shatters the quiet of the valley when they flit from pool to pool, sounds much like an ailing automatic transmission on an old car. Kingfishers seem to be constantly on the move up and down the stream, and it is hard to find one that will sit still long enough to take a good picture of it. I am still trying to get one I can be proud of.

The creek bears left toward a distant ridge where three power lines lead toward some buildings that are set well back from the channel on that side. There is still no appreciable deep water, except on the outside of a few bends and around some logs that interrupt the flow of the creek. Still, I have caught quite a few smallmouth here by being very careful and quiet.

When the channel hits the ridge ahead it swings to the right in a mile-long section that runs through much more heavily wooded country. The creek splashes through some rocky rapids a short distance above its junction with a small bluff. The water does not deepen until you come to a large, flat rock that sits out in the stream along the base of the ridge to the left.

There is a small cave two hundred yards down the straight stretch beyond the end of the curve. It is only about five feet high at the entrance and has a small vertical crack leading up from the ceiling. The cave goes farther back than the fifteen feet I cared to explore in such cramped quarters. Many lush ferns cover the slope below the cave mouth, and the area is damp with dripping water even in dry spells.

A half mile farther on, a large rock outcropping covered with red lichens deflects the current to the right. There is deeper water in occasional pockets along the base of the ridge below this point. Wood ducks seem to love this bit of woodland. I have seen more than a dozen at a time splashing up from the water ahead of me, shattering the quiet with their squealing cries.

Downstream a steep rock wall bulges out into the channel several hundred yards above the next curve. A large cave mouth yawns invitingly in the steep slope to the left. The cave is close by the creek, and its entrance is roughly triangular, eighteen feet tall at the vertex and fifteen feet across at its base. A roomy chamber with a sharply lowering ceiling leads back well beyond the light that spills in from the outside. A little below the cave, a rock with a sharp-cornered prow sticks out from the hillside into the stream.

Do not try to save any time by cutting across the woods at the beginning of the bend you can see ahead of you. This is private land, and there is a cabin sitting atop the steep bank on the left. It is hidden back in the trees, and the fields and outbuildings of a ranch lie in the large pastures only a short distance beyond.

The heights gradually flatten out around the curve below the cave. A high dirt bank stands on the right at the foot of the ridge forcing the creek into this sharp bend. The fishing is usually good in the deeper areas around this curve and through the straight section beyond. The stream bears far away from the heights on the right, but a high-water channel runs over against the base of the hillside. It is an easy, interesting hike down the channel. The caves and overhanging ledges that border it call for a little exploration in that direction either now or on your trip back up. There is one cave opening at the downstream end of the ridge that seems rather large from far below, but the climb is too treacherous for anyone to attempt when alone.

Across the valley that enters from the right is another ridge set back from the creek in the woods. It could be quite interesting when leaves are off the trees so that it can be seen more clearly. The ridge angles in toward the creek and forms a bare rock cliff that rises straight out of the water a hundred feet overhead at its highest point.

There is much deep water at the beginning of this cliff, but it shoals noticeably toward its lower end. There is another, slightly lower ridge on the opposite side of the creek a quarter of a mile away across a grassy field. A small road runs along its base, and it would be an interesting diversion to walk back along this trail as you return upstream.

The creek now bears sharply right as it comes up against a forty-foot wall of rock with some deep water at its base. The bluff quickly tapers into an open pasture, and the stream runs straight ahead into a small cliff. Here it forms a right-angle pool that bends sharply to the left in the deepest, greenest water so far. For several hundred yards the channel is reasonably straight, with quiet water along a steep slope on the right. There is a wide, long pasture on the left, and a red barn and a house stand along a county road skirting the far side of the field. The field is interrupted by a small line of trees along a gully, opening up again past the trees toward a beautiful, rock-crested ridge in the distance.

Nearing the end of the second part of the pasture, you will come to a low-water bridge on a little county road. As is frequently the case, there is a deep pool below the bridge caused by the swirling action of the water as it drops over the concrete structure. After the next turn the creek runs beneath one of the prettiest bluffs on Fox Creek. The top of the ridge it fronts is a hundred fifty feet higher than the creek bed, according to contour maps. The lower portion angles off to a fifteen-foot-high rock face that drops straight toward the water. A thick patch of scouring rushes grows at its base.

Scouring rushes are reasonably common along Ozark streams and deserve their appropriate name. They resemble two-foot-high, miniature canes that do not have any noticeable leaves. The jointed stems are soft and hollow, and they contain the plant's chlorophyll. Settlers learned long ago that these stems contain many abrasive silicon particles that made them ideal for scrubbing hard-to-clean cooking utensils.

Fox Creek swings left where a big field opens up above the right bank. There is deep water on the next bend before it becomes shallow in a straight run that intersects Bryant Creek at a downstream angle a short distance ahead. The mouth of Fox Creek is no more than half a mile below the low-water bridge back upstream.

Bryant Creek has a much greater flow than Fox Creek, and it can often be too deep to wade at this point. If possible, however, you should hike downstream to the first sharp bend below the mouth of Fox Creek. There is a towering ridge along this curve with a bare rock cap near its top that climbs over two hundred feet above the valley floor. Highway 95 runs along the ridge crest a short distance before it drops down to the Bryant Creek crossing. Deep, green water flanks the base of the ridge in a big, fish-filled pool.

If water conditions and time permit, you can cross to the far side of Bryant Creek and make your way down to the mouth of Spring Creek in about an hour. Spring Creek is a beautiful, ice-cold trout stream that flows through a steep-sided valley into Bryant Creek from the west. Chapter 24 describes a hike from Highway 95 up Bryant Creek to the mouth of Spring Creek and on to the trout ranch at Rockbridge.

MAP 12

Bryant Creek

(Chapter 23)

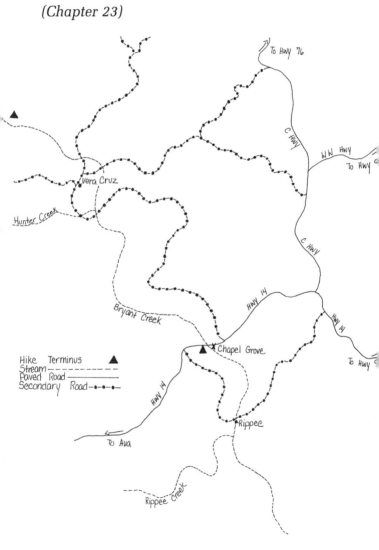

To Hwy 76

C Hwy

W W Hwy
To Hwy

Vera Cruz

Hunter Creek

C Hwy

Bryant Creek

Hwy 14

Hike Terminus ▲
Stream — — — — — —
Paved Road ——————
Secondary Road —•—•—

Chapel Grove

Hwy 14

Hwy 14

To Hwy

To Ava

Rippee

Rippee Creek

23

BRYANT CREEK ══════════════════

Above Highway 14
(Map 12)

Bryant Creek is at times one of the best small-mouth streams in the state of Missouri. Maintaining a substantial flow even during the driest of periods, the lower reaches of the stream are better traveled by canoe. Above Highway 14 there is some canoeing, but the lower average depth through here limits their traffic in the summer. To reach this section of the creek, take Highway 95 south for twenty-one miles from Mountain Grove and turn west on Highway 14. Go west on Highway 14 for eight miles to the highway bridge over the creek at Chapel Grove Gospel Music Park.

A county road turns north seventy-five yards short of the Highway 14 bridge and runs between several houses, looking much like a private drive as it goes by a large sign for Thornridge Farms. It runs parallel to the creek for a mile and then turns up a steep ridge to the right. Dropping back down to stream level after a mile or so, it crosses over the creek on low-water bridges two times on its way up the valley. The road sign at its intersection with Highway 14 has been missing for a long while, and I have been unable to get its number. Hikes up Bryant Creek could originate at either of the low-water bridges along this road if you would like to walk a shorter distance or go farther up the stream where it is smaller and there are fewer people.

To get to the lower starting point, pass over the Highway 14 bridge past the Gospel Music Park and turn left into the parking area at the west end. This turnoff is steep and can be very muddy in wet weather. If that is the case, it would be better to go back to the county road just mentioned and park at the first pull-off against the stream.

The creek runs shallow above the bridge for two hundred yards or more, with spots against the east bank that may contain a few fish. Transmission lines cross overhead at bluffs that rise eighty to a hundred feet above the right bank and have an interesting projection bulging out at their crest. The deep water a short distance upstream is filled with longear sunfish in the spring and summer.

Above this hole the creek swings back to the left in a wide, shallow run. There is no deep water until the outside of the curve that turns toward a wooded bluff on the west side. After another shallow riffle and a sharp bend to the right, you will see a long field north of the stream. The ridge that ran close to the left of the creek now angles across to the other side of this pasture. Around the curve is a low-water bridge and a deep hole immediately downstream. It has been scoured out by the current that sweeps over the bridge when the creek is flooded. This bridge is on a private road that branches off the county road paralleling the creek.

The owners of the property around the bridge may frequently be found swimming in the deep water below it in the summer. I met them in July of 1991, and we talked for a few minutes about the creek and the points of attraction along it. When they found that I was interested, they took me on a private tour of a beautiful cave and spring that lie in a shaded nook against the curve of the ridge to the north.

The spring runs from a wide, shallow cave near the top of the slope and tumbles down through a long metal flume to drop into a small overshot water wheel. The water splashes from the wheel into a shaded pool that is held back by a small concrete dam. The water in this spring and in the pool below is extremely cold, and the entire area around it is delightfully cool even in the hottest weather. One of the largest patches of wild yellow impatiens I have ever seen grows below the pool and along its overflow. Remember that this is a private spot, and you must ask permission of the owners before wandering onto their property. Their house lies at the far end of the field against the ridge at the east end.

Another spring runs from the ridge above the house and serves as the source of its water, which runs into the house through a gravity feed system that does not even use a pump. Many springs in the Ozarks are polluted, and you should never drink from any of them without treating the water; apparently, however, this one is safe. The stream from the spring flows into the creek well around the next bend to the left.

Immediately above the low-water bridge, the creek runs straight along the full length of the field to the north. A high wooded bluff parallels the water on the right with a beautiful cornice on its face that bulges far out from the vertical rock beneath it. There is deep water all along this section on the bluff side. An even deeper hole has been hollowed out on the outside of the sharp bend to the left at the end of the ridge. Above this corner a power line crosses toward the house at the edge of the field you just passed. A small branch leads back toward the spring above the house.

Bryant Creek now curves back and forth through gravel bars and an open field on the right. There are some undercut dirt banks here that sometimes have water beneath them deep enough to contain large fish. As the stream straightens out toward a house and barns, look high up on your left at the steep pasture that has been cleared atop the ridge.

The channel runs over to the base of that ridge, where it forms a wonderful green pool against a high rock bluff. This pool is the largest and deepest in the upper reaches of Bryant Creek. Upstream is another low-water bridge, at a little community called Vera Cruz; this is the first bridge on the county road leading off of Highway 14. There are popular swimming spots above and below this bridge that can yield fish if no people are around. "Keep Out" signs hang on the fence bordering the road to the right of the creek, so stay in the water or on the gravel bars when you are crossing the road. Above the bridge you can take a little lane that leads off the county road and along the left bank of the stream for a few hundred yards, or you can wade and fish the moderate holes upstream of the low-water bridge if there are no swimmers present.

A quarter of a mile beyond the low-water bridge, at the end of the small dirt road along the streambed, Hunter Creek adds its clear waters to the main stream. Draining the deep valleys to the west, Hunter Creek is also worth your time when water levels are high enough. A parking area along the county road is near the mouth of Hunter Creek, where the two streams swirl together in a deep hole that is another favorite of swimmers.

There is little deep water from Hunter Creek to the next low-water bridge, a half mile or less upstream. This bridge is the next crossing of the county road and can be reached by driving past Vera Cruz, over Hunter Creek and beyond the field where the Vera Cruz flea market is held. Good parking spots lie to the east of the bridge. Slightly upstream, watch for the tall concrete supports of the old elevated bridge that once crossed Bryant Creek. The most noticeable pier is a short distance out in the water on the left; the support on the right is up near the top of the bank and partially obscured by bushes.

A tall wooded bluff rises from the creek above the old bridge, and the stream moves toward a ridge in the distance. There are a few good fishing spots along the small ledges that stand three or four feet above normal water levels. After a couple of small curves with some deep water on their outside edges, a spring branch enters from the east and splashes into another deep pool.

You can follow this little stream about seventy-five yards into the woods to the spot the spring flows out from under some large rocks. All around the spring you will find large numbers of spice bushes, some of them as tall as twelve feet. Spice bushes have smooth bark, shiny leaves, and small berries that turn a bright red in September. All parts of the plant give off a pleasant, spicy scent when crushed between your fingers. A cave going back several yards into the hillside lies at the base of the bluff only a few yards into the woods.

Farther upstream Bryant Creek runs straight and shallow for over a hundred yards. An attractive cabin with a large brick chimney stands a few yards back from the high bank to the left. Beyond this cabin an especially noisy spring roars into the creek from the opposite side, coming in just above two deep holes where I almost always catch one or two big fish.

Follow the little waterfall of the spring back up the dirt bank and fifteen to twenty yards into the woods. There you will find the source of its water. There is no actual pool there, just a flat area twenty feet across in which the water rises through the ground, never lying more than two inches deep.

The more common orange variety of wild impatiens grows in fair numbers along the spring's outlets. One of these outlets, the larger one that goes over the noisy little fall, flows out on the upstream side of the seepage area. Another smaller channel drains out the opposite side and enters the creek slightly downstream. Across an old fence behind the spring you will find a faint road that leads up the valley parallel to the creek. It runs through woods and along overgrown fields, returning to the stream in about a mile. If you want to walk upstream along this road, keep to your left at its intersection with another narrow dirt lane a few yards back into the woods. Most of the creek from the spring to the point this road rejoins the creek is shallow and the scenery unremarkable.

The next good fishing holes are at least another mile beyond the spring. If you hike up the creek, there is little deep water and only a few moderate rock formations for the next mile and a half. The stream winds easily back and forth through gentle runs and pretty enough ridges, but I hardly ever catch any fish here.

At the first extreme bend to the right is an open field on the left over which you can see some buildings on the edge of the woods. In a short distance the little road described earlier comes in from the right and crosses into the overgrown field. Notice the depth of the cut in the bank where the road makes its way up the left bank. It has seen considerable travel in the past.

A few yards upstream on the left side you will see a large flow of water entering the stream from a patch of woods on the edge of the field. It is a little overgrown in warm weather, but walk up the little branch until you come to its source in about fifty yards. This cold spring bubbles up from a pit about fifteen feet across in a large bed of sand. The force of the water as it surges up from beneath the ground makes the yellow-white sand bubble and roll in several vents that—except for the difference in temperature—remind me of some of the springs in Yellowstone National Park. I haven't had the nerve to check my theory, but I am almost sure that the sand in the spring is quicksand. The spring alone would make this hike worthwhile.

The creek gets smaller and smaller for the next mile. The next spot of interest is at a dirt cutbank on the left where the creek swings sharply to the right. The small rock formations all over the streambed beyond the bend are especially attractive. Around the sharp curve past these rocks, walk up the wide gravel bar and look for the large dead sycamore that leans out over the water ahead of you. The impressive nest of a red-tailed hawk clings securely to its upper limbs. I just missed getting a picture of the hawk sitting beside the nest on my last trip, but I was too slow getting my camera focused. The nest is in good repair now and is presently being used, though the sycamore could fall in any flood.

Within a half mile there are two good pools, which

come as somewhat of a surprise after all the shallow water you have hiked along. Fishing is very good here even in the summer. The valley is wide and open ahead, and I am sure there are interesting spots to visit ahead. This is as far as I have ever hiked, but there is no reason for you not to explore further on your own.

MAP 13

Spring Creek–Rockbridge

(Chapter 24)

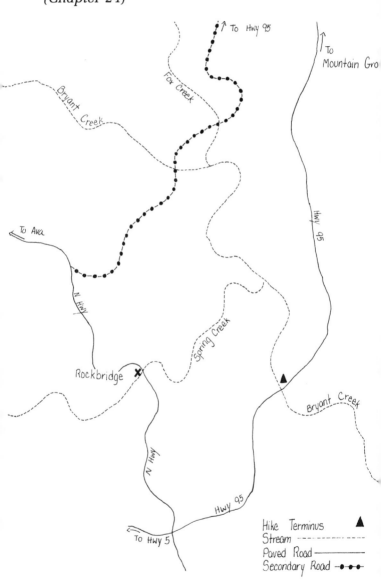

24

SPRING CREEK

Bryant Creek to Rockbridge
(Map 13)

Of all the waterways with the name "Spring Creek" that I have fished and hiked in the Ozarks, this one comes closest to my idea of what such a creek should look like. The springs here supply icy cold, mineral-laden water that passes a succession of dark, beautiful bluffs, open fields, and wooded ridges: the perfect setting for a short, lovely creek.

Heavy mists often hang close over sheltered portions of this stream as humid air is chilled when it moves slowly above the frigid water. The fogs of a misty day and the still dampness of early morning or late afternoon can create an unforgettable, eerie atmosphere for a hike along Spring Creek.

The Rainbow Trout Ranch at Rockbridge, near the N Highway crossing of Spring Creek, puts rainbow trout into its area of the stream. Some fugitives from the ranch inhabit the lower reaches of the creek. Trout may be found all the way down to its mouth and a short distance into Bryant Creek. The lower part of this hike is along a portion of Bryant Creek that flows by several large pools and two high bluffs. Its large flow is harder to wade than Spring Creek and can only be attempted when water levels are low.

The hike should be planned as a round trip from the Highway 95 bridge over Bryant Creek. The Rainbow Trout Ranch at the upper end has diverted much of the creek through large ponds on its land. You should not fish there unless you talk to the people at Rockbridge and make some arrangement with them. If you can arrange for passage through the ranch, a car could be left there and one at the lower end.

The bridge over Bryant Creek lies twenty-eight miles south of Mountain Grove on Highway 95, about seven miles past the Highway 14 intersection. For the last couple of miles before the highway drops down to the valley, it runs along a precipitous ridge that parallels the creek two hundred fifty feet below. This ridge tops the same high bluff you will see towering over you if you take the hike down to the mouth of Fox Creek (see chapter 22).

You can also reach your starting point by driving east from Ava on Highway 14 for twenty-four miles to Highway 95 and then turning south to the creek. There was no sign on the Bryant Creek bridge the last time I passed by. If it is still missing when you look for it, don't be concerned about having found the right spot. Bryant Creek is the only stream with any but a minimal flow that crosses the highway for many miles in either direction.

To get to Rockbridge and the Rainbow Trout Ranch, go two miles west of the Bryant Creek bridge on Highway 95 to N Highway and turn north for two miles to the Spring Creek bridge. The buildings, dam, houses, and old mill at Rockbridge lie down a paved road at the sign northwest of the bridge. Even if you don't plan to take this hike, you should treat yourself to a drive down to Rockbridge any time you are in the area.

There are several parking spots on the upstream side of the Highway 95 bridge over Bryant Creek. Be careful to keep from getting stuck in the loose gravel if you park on the bars, and beware of flash flooding if you are close to the creek. Should rain be in the forecast, park in one of the areas higher up.

There is plenty of deep water along a high bluff at the

beginning of the hike. This pool bends to the right at a slough on the bluff side, continuing on with more deep water above the curve. I almost stepped on a small soft-shell turtle while fording the creek here. It was burrowing frantically under the rocks as I approached and I would never have noticed it except for the little disturbance it made as it dug itself in. When it lay still, it was amazing how well the little turtle was hidden. I wonder how many well-camouflaged animals such as this I have passed close by through the years as they lay concealed within a few feet of me. Compared to the hundreds I have seen, the number would certainly be startling.

The creek now narrows along another bluff that is stained with red and black streaks from mineral seepage. There are some indications of possible caves up high. I have only been here in summer when the trees make it difficult to see the rock surface completely, and the thick undergrowth has discouraged me from exploring that side of the stream. The gravel bars are thickly overgrown with scrub trees, and there are frequent patches of large cane along both banks.

Above a shallow riffle you again have flat fields back of the trees on the banks. Two hundred yards or more of water up to waist deep lies upstream, with hardly any way to bypass it on the banks unless you are fond of thick bushes and high weeds. The field on the left parallels the creek for over a mile with a county road on its far side. There are some trails below the high-water bank of the creek in the woods along this field.

Beyond the fields Bryant Creek runs toward a high wooded ridge far ahead. It is crowned with two lines of exposed rock near its summit. Soon the creek splits around an island, the main channel running to the right. The left side is dry in low water but seems to be getting deeper every year. It may eventually become the main channel as it is deepened by the scouring action of flood waters.

An ATV road on the next bar leads off to the left toward the county road about a quarter of a mile away. If you pause and let things get quiet, you can hear the cars high above you where Highway 95 parallels this part of the creek along the ridgetop to your right. When the water gets too deep to wade, go up the hill to the left and find the trail through the woods. Follow it until you come to a large, dry channel that crosses in front of you. Turn down this channel to the creek.

After you have taken many hikes along Ozark streams in the summer, you will know that one of the most common weeds in the low areas of the shaded woods has stems covered with short, stinging hairs. These weeds cause a severe burning reaction when you brush against them, and they can attack your skin through any but the thickest pants. The irritation they cause is painful, but it will fade in ten minutes or less without lasting effects. You should do your best to avoid them, but sometimes the creek forces you to cut through spots where they are thick. Knock them down with your staff and step on their stems; bend them away from you and hope they don't pop back up and strike you before you move on. I have my own names for this weed, but my book on poisonous plants politely calls it the wood nettle.

On one hike early in September, I saw something of a more pleasant nature growing along the west bank of this part of Bryant Creek. Dangling from a thick mass of vines, with leaves virtually indistinguishable from those of wild grapes, were hundreds of tassels of something that looked very much like the pictures of hops I had seen. Checking my references on herbs when I got home, I found that this is exactly what they are. When I read of their use as a sedative and a tonic, in addition to their being a flavoring for beer, I was sorry I hadn't picked any of the papery, conelike hops to take home with me. If you are there in the right season, be on the lookout for them.

When you get down to the creek at the mouth of the dry tributary, wade over to the bar on the right side and walk up along the pool that bends gradually to the left. Cross back over when the water shallows. Bordering the slope on the right on the edge of the next long stretch of deep water, several large rocks commonly shelter a few large fish in the shadows around them.

Bryant Creek swings to the right past this long pool and runs along a gravel bar that boasts thick stands of cardinal flowers in August and September. Spring Creek enters from the left and pours into a deep pool midway along this bend. The cold water from Spring Creek makes it possible for some trout to inhabit this hole. You can feel the big difference in temperature as you leave the comparative warmth of Bryant Creek and wade into the flow of the smaller stream.

A little cabin is hidden back out of sight in the thick woods on the northwest side of the creek mouth. There are no posted signs along the banks, but you should respect private property by staying in the creek. The flow of Spring Creek is shallow, cold, and swift for several hundred yards above its mouth, and there is more watercress all along the banks of this stream than I have seen anywhere else in the Ozarks. Watercress usually grows in and a short distance below many springs, but on Spring Creek it is present along its entire length, sometimes in patches that cover entire bars like a carpet. Deer love to feed on the cress, and it is not at all unusual to come upon them here while they are browsing with their heads down. The splashing sound of the rushing water nearby masks the noise of your approach, making it easier for you to get close.

In still areas of the creek, there is an abundance of duckweed, a tiny plant that resembles a thick scum of moss or algae. It floats on the surface, sometimes in extensive rafts, and doesn't have distinct stems or leaves, just small fleshy masses of cells. Duckweed is an important food for muskrat and other small animals, including ducks. Not too surprisingly, Spring Creek supports a healthy population of wood ducks.

The channel flows far away from any steep slopes in its lower reaches, winding in shallow runs through a rocky bed. The first deep water is along the base of a ridge that angles in from the left, with a twenty-foot bluff dropping off into the creek. There is a wide field to the right that the stream curves gradually around.

A no-trespassing sign warns you away from the left bank before the creek turns from the ridge and splits around a big bar. A long, straight run flows against a rugged cliff rising straight out of the water upstream, and a road crosses short of this vertical mass of rock, near a two-wire electric service. The portion of the road turning off to your right leads back to the cabin at the mouth of the creek, but don't follow it because the little lane is posted.

The valley is narrow and thickly wooded at this mottled bluff. The darkly shaded face of the cliff looms high over the water above a long, gradual curve. Some small caves are in evidence behind the dense foliage. The creek is filled with big boulders and deep pockets of water that are scattered through bright, splashing rapids beneath the cliff. The curve tightens as the bluff finally lowers and the creek widens into a long hole of moderate depth.

Immediately above this pool a bluff of a totally different character rises along the left bank. Running straight for two hundred yards, it is commonly bathed in sunlight and presents a much more cheerful face toward the creek. The upstream end of this bluff is joined by another slope that angles up to meet it along a trail-like ledge. The two inclines meet at a small pothole of a cave about thirty yards back from the water. The creek sweeps away to the right at a deep pool that is bordered by a raft of duckweed when the water is low.

The channel now winds back and forth into a large open area that may at first appear to be an old field but is actually a wide, overgrown bar that the creek skirts on the right. An actual field begins across the far bank and parallels the stream channel for almost a mile. The volume of the creek's flow seems somehow greater here as it flows knee-deep through a wide run. On my last trip I caught and released a sixteen-inch rainbow trout in the deeper water about a hundred yards upstream. Several more trout followed the one I caught as I brought it in, but I couldn't get any more to strike.

A spring flows into Spring Creek from the right two-thirds of the way up the open field. The water enters the main stream with a noisy splashing, making it easy to find if you wade up that bank and head toward the noise. The spring originates far across the pasture, along the base of the ridge in the distance. It flows through a culvert under the faint road that travels the length of the field.

Soon the creek divides into two channels along an attractive tree-covered bluff, and you can see a large open area ahead. The smaller portion of the stream to the left is the original, natural channel. The right branch is the combination of three outlet channels from the large dirt-banked ponds at Rainbow Trout Ranch. Most of the flow of the stream has been diverted through these ponds. You should end your hike short of the developed area of the trout ranch unless you have made arrangements with the people at Rockbridge to pass through their land.

MAP 14

James River

(Chapter 25)

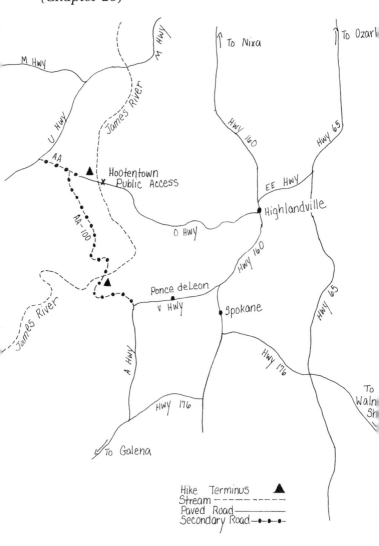

M HWY

M HWY

To Nixa

To Ozark

James River

U HWY

HWY 160

HWY 65

AA

Hootentown
Public Access

EE HWY

Highlandville

AA-100

O HWY

HWY 160

James River

Ponce de Leon

HWY 65

V HWY

Spokane

A HWY

HWY 176

HWY 65

To
Waln
Sh

HWY 176

To Galena

Hike Terminus
Stream ------
Paved Road
Secondary Road —•—•—

25

JAMES RIVER ═══════════════════

Old Steel Bridge to Hootentown
(Map 14)

Although the James River in this section is somewhat large for easy wading, it is still one of my favorite spots to hike and fish. There are large gravel bars and convenient trails that can be used to skirt the extremely deep areas, and I have completed this hike with great pleasure many times over the past twenty-one years. The fishing is usually good in this stretch of the river when water conditions are right. One of the last of Missouri's picturesque steel bridges crosses the river here, and one of the two largest natural bridges in the state stands high above the river downstream from the new Hootentown Bridge.

To drive to this portion of the James River, go south from Springfield on U.S. Highway 160 past Nixa to Highlandville. One-fourth of a mile beyond EE, turn right on O and follow it for six miles to the river. A couple of miles down O is a small trout farm in a sheltered valley where a cold spring gushes out of a hillside to the north of the road.

The pavement ends and after a quarter mile of gravel road, O crosses the river on a new concrete bridge. I was more than a little upset when I made my trip to the river while preparing for this chapter and found that the old steel-truss Hootentown Bridge was gone. Much of the charm of this hike, in the past, was that it began and ended at one of these delightful bridges.

A number of the beautiful, aging bridges in the Ozarks have been torn down and replaced by new and safer concrete structures in the past few years. I know the old bridges needed to be replaced, but the new versions are boringly utilitarian and lack the character and charm of their ancestors. When it comes time for the last few of the old breed to be decommissioned, I hope some bureaucrat or engineer is sensitive enough to leave the precious antiques in place as a tribute to the past. It seems to me that it would be easy enough to route the new bridge close by without tearing the old one down.

There is a large parking area with rest rooms and river access for boat launching on the upstream side at the west end of the new bridge. If you are making this a one-way hike, a vehicle can be left here. No overnight camping is allowed in this public-use area. On the downstream side of the bridge, the old stands of trees have been cleared for a canoe rental business and attendant buildings. I was concerned about the increased volume of canoe traffic on the river due to the rental concession at Hootentown, but on a recent Wednesday afternoon in late July I didn't see any canoes in six hours of hiking. Plan your trip during the week and in times of low water if you want solitude, but I doubt that the number of floaters is ever overwhelming. If the water is too high or the weather too cold for wading, go to the Hootentown Bridge and rent a canoe.

If you don't feel up to a long hike and don't want to rent a canoe, you might want to drive down to the old steel bridge to take some photographs and then go back up to Hootentown to see the natural bridge. High up on the first wooded ridge downstream of the parking area, the huge stone arch stands near the top of the slope. With every passing year, the trees get taller and the bridge is hidden more and more from the observer down at river level. It can best be seen when the leaves have fallen.

If you are hiking along the river in summer and find it hard to locate the bridge, look for the shallow channel cut into the steep slope by the runoff of rainwater sluicing beneath the arch. Follow this channel up the face of the incline, and you should find the trails made by other hikers. The arch was formed along a fracture a few yards back from the edge of the cliff face. It was enlarged by weathering and erosion until its separation from the rest of the ridge now ranges from one to twelve feet along its eighty-foot span. The top is quite flat and its five- to twenty-foot width is easy to cross safely. When atop the bridge, you stand some sixty feet above the lower side of its supporting columns.

Trails lead down to this formation from the top of the ridge, off County Road AA–100. This little road is the first turn to the left from AA Highway west of Hootentown. The access from the road is currently posted against trespassing, due in great part I am sure to a fatal fall there in 1975. I have never seen the riverbank posted, but look for signs in case the situation changes. The view across the river valley from the top of the span is sensational and well worth the climb of one hundred fifty feet from stream level.

To get to the river access farther downstream, cross the Hootentown Bridge and take the gravel road to the left at the T intersection. Follow this narrow lane until it intersects a blacktop road, AA Highway, at the top of a steep hill. The dirt road splits into a Y just before it reaches AA for no obvious reason—either route will take you where you want to go. Turn to the left on AA to County Road AA–100, where another left turn will take you past Steel Bridge Estates and back to the river. AA–100 turns sharply left across the river on the old steel bridge at the bottom of the hill where V–70 goes straight ahead. This old bridge of my memories still stands, but who knows how long it will remain. The load limit in July of 1991 was posted as only eight tons, an indication of its weakened condition.

Cross the bridge on its wooden planking to the east side of the river. There is a parking area immediately to the left as you leave the bridge, but go upstream to the point the road turns away to the right. On your left is a small turnoff with a trail that leads to an old ford across the river. This is a good point to begin your hike.

As I mentioned earlier, water depths here are consistently greater than those of most streams described in this book. There are many points at which you must leave the river and skirt long, deep holes. The fishing is usually good below the long, swift runs and rapids; splashing water seems to supply the extra oxygen that smallmouth need in the warmer waters of summer. Live bait drifted slowly through deeper holes, whether on the bottom or suspended under a float, can yield good mixed catches of bass, goggle-eye, catfish, drum, and several varieties of sunfish.

If you are wading up from the old steel bridge, the first stretch of water is very wide and moderately shallow. You must keep looking ahead of you for areas that can be waded easily. The deeper water switches unpredictably from one side of the river to the other, and your path upstream will have to zigzag correspondingly. Sometimes it helps to get up on a high bank and look down at the stream to spot crossings and good pools that might contain fish. I have caught many smallmouth and largemouth from the river halfway up the first ridge to the east.

The first curve ahead of you is a very long arc of one and a half to two miles, with open pasture and corn fields along the west bank. Past this curve a wooded area closes in on the left, and there is a private camp very close to the river immediately above a ten- to fifteen-foot bank. A pleasant little spring branch enters above this camp and is a good spot for a short excursion to the side.

The river now bends to the right and gets swifter and shallower in splashing rills. A two-wire service line crosses on a gentle curve to the left where open fields predominate on the east side of the valley. A wide road comes down to the river beyond this curve beneath a cleared hillside. Rock outcroppings along a high ridge above this bare hill become progressively higher and more impressive as you go upstream, while the river continues its gentle swing to the west. There are some spots where there may be caves high among the rocks on this ridge, but I have never crossed the river here to explore.

Winding back and forth across the valley, the James flows over exposed rock layers for a short distance in the best rapids on this part of the river. It comes up against a high, heavily wooded ridge on the left in another mile. Make certain you are on the west bank at this point if you wish to climb to the Hootentown Natural Bridge. The water in the river is far too deep to wade across if you wait until you get opposite the arch. In warm weather the vegetation is very dense along this bank and walking will be quite hard. For this reason and because the visibility of the arch is much better later in the year, this part of the hike is much better after the first frosts in the fall.

From the natural bridge the river runs more or less straight for just over a mile, with occasional spots where the fishing can be quite good. In mid to late summer, keep an eye on the shaded sandbars and low banks for the large flowers of the rose mallow. Most mallows in this area are white, but some are pink to light rose. The plants stand five to six feet tall and have five-inch, purple-centered flowers that look very much like their close relative the hibiscus. This mallow is much more common in marshy areas farther south, where it is commonly called the marsh mallow. The confection by that name was originally made from a base of a sticky substance taken from the roots of these flowers.

The riverbanks upstream of the natural bridge are quite open, and it is easy for you to see that you are approaching the new Hootentown Bridge. Fish the long straight runs in this area carefully. Through the years I have caught several smallmouth in the deeper water along these banks. Cross the river on the riffle at the curve below the bridge and exit near the boat-launching section of the public-use area on the west side.

MAP 15

Bull Creek

(Chapter 26)

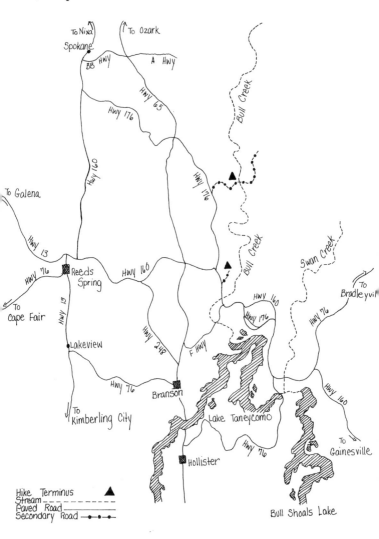

To Nixa
To Ozark
Spokane
BB HWY
A HWY
HWY 65
Hwy 176
Bull Creek
Hwy 160
To Galena
HWY 13
Reeds
Spring
HWY 176
HWY 160
HWY 176
Bull Creek
Swan Creek
HWY 13
To
Cape Fair
HWY 160
To
Bradleyvil
HWY 176
HWY 176
HWY 76
Lakeview
HWY 248
F HWY
HWY 160
HWY 76
Branson
To
Kimberling City
Lake Taneycomo
HWY 160
To
Gainesville
HWY 76
Hollister
Bull Shoals Lake

Hike Terminus ▲
Stream ---
Paved Road ———
Secondary Road ●-●-●

26

BULL CREEK ═══════════════════════

Above Walnut Shade
(Map 15)

       Bull Creek is a haven of quiet and solitude in the midst of the well-traveled and rapidly growing tourist area near Branson. Although more and more houses are being built on the slopes of its watershed, a few minutes walk from any bridge will take you quickly away from civilization to the haunts of deer, beavers, and water birds. Water levels vary extremely with the seasons and so does the fishing, but I have made trips to Bull Creek when the fishing was as good as I have experienced anywhere. Smallmouth, goggle-eye, and longear sunfish are common, and when water temperatures are right, an occasional trout will wander up from Lake Taneycomo, the creek's final destination. The valley through which the stream flows is surprisingly wide and the ridges around it are only moderately steep. There are no towering bluffs or spectacular geologic features along its course. Bull Creek's attractions are its fishing and the peaceful, quiet beauty of its water.

To reach this area, follow Highway 65 south from Springfield, proceeding some fifteen miles south of Ozark to Highway 176. Turn left on 176 for about two miles to the first county road on the left, which leads off the highway at the crest of a ridge before a sharp right turn. This will take you to the creek and the parking spots at the upper end of the hike. The county road sign was missing at the highway intersection when I last visited the spot, but I am sure the number is 176–30. This county road leads along and down the side of a ridge, finally crossing Bull Creek at a low-water bridge. There are several parking spots on either side of the stream. Leave a vehicle here if you are making this a one-way hike.

The starting point of the hike can be reached by going down 176 past the 176–30 turnoff to the intersection with Highway 160. (If you are going to this spot directly from Springfield or Ozark, it is better to turn directly off Highway 65 onto 160, about three miles south of 176.) Take 160 to the bridge over Bull Creek at Walnut Shade.

Turn left immediately before you get to the creek onto a county road that angles off to the north of the bridge and turns upstream as it gets closer to the creek. This road is quite rough above Walnut Shade, leading over several areas of uneven ledges and broken rock, but ordinary passenger cars do make the drive quite commonly. Portions of it can be very muddy and have deep ruts in wet weather. If the lower portions of this road are impassable, park near the Highway 160 bridge. Your hike will be longer and start on an undistinguished portion of the creek, but it is better not to attempt a section of the road that is doubtful.

This rough little track goes upstream for about a mile to a low-water bridge that crosses over to private property on the far side. Park in the short pull-off that is straight ahead of you where the road turns sharply right across the bridge. Bull Creek runs shallow and wide for several hundred yards above this spot. Don't become impatient because of the long stretches of undistinguished water— there are many deep pools ahead.

The streambed is composed of wide, flat layers of rock to a point well upstream from here. It is especially slippery and you should be cautious while wading. The little bend to the right curves around an unusual weathered rock

Giant clusters of cruel thorns guard the trunk of a honey locust tree, one of many along the North Fork upstream from Topaz Mill.

A large beaver pond far up Indian Creek. Note the beaver lodge in the right center of the photograph.

The high triangular mouth of the lower cave on Fox Creek.

A lone morel mushroom growing in a patch of spring wildflowers along Fox Creek.

The first of many striking bluffs on Bryant Creek.

A frothing spring gushes out among watercress and jewelweed to plunge noisily into Bryant Creek above Highway 14.

Old mill building and dam at Rockbridge on Spring Creek near Ava on N Highway.

Hodgson's Mill and its spring. The spring branch flows into lower Bryant Creek a short distance away.

Steel bridge over the James River during a summer thunderstorm.

Rapids and small falls on Bull Creek a short distance above the Highway 160 bridge at Walnut Shade.

Heavy snow blankets Bull Creek at the Walnut Shade bridge.

A deer family cautiously crossing Bull Creek on a gravel bar above Walnut Shade.

Richland Falls on Richland Creek near the Buffalo River in
Arkansas.

House-size boulders blocking the streambed in Richland Creek
upstream of the Richland Creek Campground in Arkansas.

ledge that is part of the creek bed when the water is high. It is worthwhile for you to walk up on the ledge to examine the rock more carefully.

Around this bend there are some private dwellings in the trees beyond the east bank. When the channel moves back to the left above the houses, there is an attractive section of rapids that is even more interesting when the water is high because the taller ledges to the right become part of the flow. Most hikers who climb up on the high banks above such shallow runs are surprised to look down and discover just how many bass are actually in these spots. Many also become frustrated in trying to figure out how to catch them. Any large fish that have backs mottled with splotches of brown are suckers—don't bother casting for them. They seldom strike a lure, though I have caught a few over the years on very small jigs.

Above the rapids is a waist-deep pool along a high wooded ridge to the left. After a gentle curve there is a rock shelf completely across the creek, which drops over it in a pretty little fall. A short distance above the ledge, an electric service line crosses toward a house well back beyond a field on the left. The creek now swings back and forth in a series of three curves with high, undercut dirt banks on the outer sides of the bends. The water scours out deep holes along these banks, and the fishing is usually good here. As the stream straightens past the last cutbank a road leads off to the left toward a two-story house a few hundred yards away. The channel then runs through shallows to the right and splits into several small branches near a ridge.

Following a swing to the left of that ridge, you can see a long, very wide section of a large gravel bar that flanks the water in the direction of another low ridge a half mile or so away. A small portion of the creek branches to the right, and there are usually some sections of fishable water there. This flow rejoins the main channel at an extremely large pool, which is backed up by a temporary dam of rock that has been scooped from the streambed and piled across the creek.

Ahead of you, part of the way around a bend to the left, a long concrete bridge crosses ten feet above the water, carrying a road that leads to private houses and a gravel operation. A small dirt road turns north upstream of the bridge on the east side, paralleling the creek for a short distance before curving back toward a private home.

Around the next bend to the right is a long pasture to the east of Bull Creek that extends for at least one and a half miles. The field is interrupted by one area of trees down close to the stream and runs in a continuous, sweeping arc behind them. The creek channel is wide and shallow at the beginning of this field, but as you go farther up there are some pockets of deep water along the ridge opposite the pasture. The landscape remains much the same beyond an ATV track that crosses upstream of the copse of trees on the right.

Metal barns and corrals come into view near the creek as you approach the end of the field. The flow of water narrows here, and there are deep, shaded pockets of water around some large rocks. I once caught one of the blackest smallmouth I have ever seen around one of these boulders. Smallmouth are usually light brown when young, growing to a mottled darker brown when older, but occasionally an extremely dark specimen will make you wonder what is on the line as you reel it in.

Another low-water bridge crosses in front before you get even with the barns, and you can see some small stands, similar to bleachers at a softball field, between the barns and the creek. Above the bridge is a deep hole from which I have caught many fish, but it is being used more and more as a swimming hole because of its proximity to the bridge. You may find it full of swimmers. Cross over to the left above that hole; the right bank is overgrown and hard to make your way along.

Soon you will come to another section of wide rock layers that line the streambed as a ridge begins to rise to the east. The channel then bends to the left and offers several deep holes among boulders on the inside of the curve. Within twenty minutes of walking along this stretch on my last trip, I encountered a splendid mink, a startled turkey hen, and three deer crossing the stream. The deer never saw me and I managed to snap a couple of pictures of them, but the mink and turkey were uncooperative. The mink dove out of sight when I moved, and the turkey put on the brakes when she saw me and flew back into the woods from which she had just emerged.

The creek now swings in a wide arc around a field to the left, and there are several pockets of deep water on the straight portion before the start of the curve. After the bend the water becomes shallow and a road leads down from some houses and barns on the left. There is a large dry wash on the right and the stream continues shallow with wide gravel bars for over two hundred yards as it leads toward a high ridge in the distance. Short of the ridge you will find the deepest hole on Bull Creek above Walnut Shade.

Around the end of this ridge, as the curve sharpens to the right, look high above you for the house on its crest. The owners must have one of the best views imaginable of the Bull Creek valley. The house is most easily seen after you have gotten completely around the bend and are on the next straight run. I spent at least fifteen minutes stalking a great egret at this curve one July and wound up with a blurred picture of something vaguely white flying away from me through the trees.

Egrets and green herons are hard to slip up on, but even more difficult is the great blue heron. This large heron tends to fly much farther than other birds do after being startled. They land so far ahead that by the time you catch up to one again, you have probably stopped stalking it so carefully. You are usually startled all over again as it gives its unlovely, croaking cry, lumbers into the air, and beats its way gracefully upstream ahead of you.

There are large boulders in this straight run, and you should take time to fish around them. I picked up a small-mouth, a largemouth, or a goggle-eye by each of the big rocks on my last hike. Back in the large pasture to the left, you will see a house and barn at its upper end. Another house is visible upstream past a thin tree line that runs perpendicular to the creek. A two-wire service line passes overhead, leading to the houses.

Soon, a big curve sweeps around to the left after a slough enters from the right, and the creek runs shallow, straight, and wide for hundreds of yards as it flows under another service line. A short distance ahead a cabin sits close above the stream atop a fifteen-foot bank, as the creek turns hard to the left at a deep pool. Convenient steps lead down from the house to a concrete landing immediately above the normal level of the still water.

This particular pool somehow manages to stay much as I first saw it over twenty years ago. Of all the spots from here down to Walnut Shade, it is the only one that is easily recognized from year to year. The ravages of weathering and erosion seem hardly to have changed it since my first trip down Bull Creek in 1969.

From here on up to your endpoint at the next low-water bridge, there is nothing extraordinary on the creek. I usually walk up a faint road that begins across from the house on the left bank and runs up to the county road by the bridge. There are some pretty pools in the next half mile above the low-water bridge if you want to walk up and take the time to fish them. Don't be surprised if you round a curve here when the rainfall has been scanty and find that the creek bed is suddenly dry. This is another of those spots where a stream disconcertingly flows underground for a short distance. A few yards of walking will bring you back to a living creek again.

MAP 16

Richland Creek

(Chapter 27)

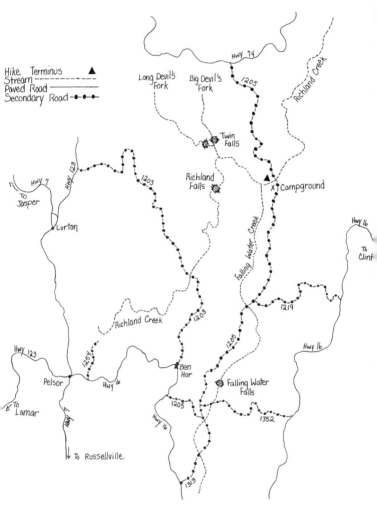

Hike Terminus ▲
Stream ------
Paved Road ————
Secondary Road •-•-•-•

Hwy 74

Long Devils Fork

Big Devil's Fork

Richland Creek

1205

Twin Falls

Richland Falls

Hwy 123

Hwy 7

To Jasper

1203

Campground

Lurton

Hwy 16

To Clint

Falling Water Creek

1219

Richland Creek

1203

Hwy 123

1254

Ben Hur

1205

Hwy 16

Falling Water Falls

Pelsor

Hwy 16

1205

1352

To Lamar

Hwy 7

1313

To Russellville

27

RICHLAND CREEK

Above Forestry Road 1205
(Map 16)

Richland Creek is one of the best-kept secrets in Arkansas. The main stream and its tributaries flow through some of the most beautiful small valleys you will find anywhere in the Ozarks. When you get away from bridges and campgrounds, the fishing is exceptional. It is amazing how few people outside of the immediate area even know of Richland Creek's existence and even more surprising how few of those who go there actually hike in to view its very special features. When you think of Richland Creek, you should think of waterfalls: in seasons when the water supply is adequate, four impressive falls await you within a four-mile radius of the campground where you park your car.

To reach your starting point, travel south from Harrison down Arkansas State Highway 7, one of the state's designated scenic routes. As it winds its way along the ridges near what is called the "Grand Canyon" of Arkansas, the spectacular views that unfold before you make it hard to keep your mind on your driving.

Unfortunately, the road isn't kind to the driver who doesn't keep his eyes on the snaky curves ahead. The smell of overheated brakes is not at all uncommon when following behind a tourist from the flatlands, and gawking drivers often slow the traffic to a crawl. Take advantage of the parking spots by the many shops and at the overlooks to stop and look at the scenery. Above all, don't be in a hurry.

Drive down Highway 7 through Jasper, which lies twenty miles south of Harrison, to Pelsor. Not really a town, Pelsor is just a store at the northwest corner of the Highway 7 intersection with Highway 123 to the west and Highway 16 to the east. This store does not stay open late, even in the tourist season. Keep this in mind if you are in need of gasoline or supplies for your hike. There are no other stores or gas stations in the immediate area.

Turn left on Highway 16 and go nine miles to Ben Hur, which is merely a tin-roofed house on a sharp curve to the right where Forestry Road 1203 leads off to the left. Before you get to Ben Hur, watch for the sign directing you south to Pedestal Rocks. These spectacularly weathered rock columns stand about a mile off the parking area adjacent to Highway 16. Make certain you allow time for a hike to the rocks on your trip.

Go beyond Ben Hur for a little over a mile on Highway 16 to Forestry Road 1205. The Richland Creek camping area lies nine miles north down the crooked and steep roadway. It is not a good idea to pull any but the smallest trailer down this twisting incline to the creek. In a short distance your route intersects a delightful, splashing stream aptly named Falling Water Creek. This small tributary of Richland Creek more than lives up to its name by dropping several hundred feet as it tumbles down its valley to intersect the larger creek west of the campground. The road moves back and forth along Falling Water Creek for several miles.

Forestry Road 1352, which leads off 1205 to the east, runs past Falling Water Church and back out to Highway 16. After you pass 1352, watch carefully for the next parking area to the right of the road. This is merely a wide place where you can pull off on the shoulder of the road adjacent to Falling Water Falls. There is a rough, steep turnoff to a parking spot above the falls, but it is safer to park in the small area parallel to the stream alongside the main road. It is easy to pass by this spot before you see the delicate cascade of the falls, so go slowly and be alert. The falls drop some ten to twelve feet over a wide ledge in a narrow, graceful arc to a large pool below. You will want to take the time to climb down below the waterfall to fully appreciate its beauty.

If you have time to stop at a few more of the scenic spots on your way down the valley, pull off into any of the frequent parking areas beside the road and walk over to the creek. You will discover attractive pools and camping areas that are often missed by the traveler who is in too much of a hurry. The scenery along Falling Water Creek alone would make this trip worthwhile, but there is much more to come when you get to Richland Creek. After the road crosses Falling Water Creek, Forestry Road 1219 comes in from the right off of Highway 16; the intersection has a sign warning that 1219 is steep and difficult. Now 1205 climbs high above the east bank of the creek and starts its final descent to the main stream after an extremely sharp curve to the right.

As Richland Creek comes into view, signs on the left direct you to the camping area on the near side of the bridge. There are many developed camping spots here, and the facilities include tables, chemical toilets, and at least one hand pump for drinking water. When the road through the campground branches, take the one to the right that goes down along the creek. Many people use this campground in the summer, and the large pools nearby are usually filled with swimmers. Your hike will take you upstream above the crowds.

There is a sign-in station at the upper end of the cleared area of the campground near the mouth of Falling Water Creek. You should fill in one of the simple questionnaires available here with information concerning your hike, a safeguard that makes it easier for you to be found in case something unforeseen happens. You should, of course, let someone know the destination and duration of any hike you attempt, wherever it may take you. The chances are that you will never need rescuing, but such precautions are never wasted effort.

A trail leads off to the west across the course of Falling Water Creek, which is dry here in midsummer, and over to the main stream. The bed of Richland Creek at this point consists of wide, flat sheets of limestone that are fissured in long diagonal cracks running upstream to the right. The main stream often flows underground through this area when there has been little rainfall.

There are pools of water around some mammoth boulders above the fractured limestone beds. Beyond them, in a bed that is choked with three- to ten-foot rocks, are many small channels and miniature waterfalls splashing their way to the pools below. The first deep hole above here is an intensely green pool surrounded by rocks the size of small houses, and the water flows into it from above through one small opening between the rocks. Scrambling up this portion of the streambed between the massive stones always makes me feel insignificant—I never regain a true perspective until I walk upstream to a point where the rocks are not so overwhelming. There are more holes of water ahead and the fishing gets better and better as you get farther from the campground.

Keep in mind that I am describing this hike after making it in a dry summer. When the water is up, this part of the creek is especially swift and full. You would then be well advised to follow the trail that crosses over to the right side of the valley and climbs high above the level of the creek. The view from portions of this trail is impressive, especially in the autumn after the leaves have fallen.

Deer and beavers are common throughout this entire watershed, and several of the beavers I have come across have shown much less fear than their cousins on other streams. Several small springs enter the creek low against the south bank, downstream of the sharp swing of the channel to the left. Looking upstream above the springs, a high bluff curves around in front of you from the right. There is an occasional beaver dam backing up the water around the point where the sheer bluff becomes covered with trees. These dams are constantly being swept away, and their existence testifies to the tenacity and stubbornness of the beavers—though it may not say much for their prudence.

Soon you will come to a large boulder with a sharp vertical edge sticking out into a deep pool that is a consistent producer of large bass. Beyond this spot a similar rock with a jagged, twenty-five-foot-high corner bulges out below another wide hole. I have caught a surprising number of big goggle-eye from this pool over the years. As the creek narrows again, it passes by a small, heavily fissured bluff on the left. The strata composing it are arranged in unusually thin layers broken by large vertical cracks. At another deeply scored bluff a few yards upstream, the channel veers sharply left and a tributary enters from directly ahead.

This occasional stream, Devil's Fork, is merely a dry wash during much of the year. If you are lucky enough to be there when it is flowing, proceed up its course for less than a quarter mile to the confluence of Big Devil's Fork and Long Devil's Fork. A short distance above the place they meet to form one stream, both creeks drop over the same ledge only a few yards from one another. Separated by the narrow rock promontory that divides the two watersheds, the Twin Falls are a breathtaking sight when viewed from just below the junction of the two creeks. If you visit the spot in times of drought, it is hard to imagine the transformation it undergoes when the falls are alive.

Only half a mile upstream of the mouth of Devil's Fork, Richland Creek has a surprise of its own. After a short, steep area of rapids above the pool at the mouth of the tributary, Richland Creek bears off to the right into a straight run that is accented by several miniature falls. Soon the stream widens into the largest pool you will find along this hike. The wide, deep hole feeds its beautiful green water down into a jumbled, broken area below its lower margin. You must skirt it on the right bank because of the steep bluff and deep water on the other side. After another short, swift stretch of tumbling water, you will come at last to Richland Falls.

These falls are active to some degree during the driest seasons, but there is a dramatic difference in the volume of the flow when the water is high. During peak water levels, Richland Falls is an unbroken torrent fifty yards wide and eight feet high. In late summer it shrinks drastically and splashes down through four or five widely isolated, narrow channels, most of the water tumbling over the far left side. There is some pretty water and scenery above the falls, but I usually end the hike here.

I first learned of Richland Falls from an article in a national outdoor magazine when I was living only a short drive to the south in Russellville. The brief article was accompanied by a photograph of a fisherman casting into a large pool beneath a high narrow ribbon of a fall. Within a week of reading the article, I got some contour maps of the area and with their help I made my way to the Richland Creek campground and walked up to the falls. I had to laugh when I compared what I saw on the creek to the picture in the magazine. The short, wide aspect of Richland Falls was nothing like the one in the photograph. Looking at the picture again when I got home, it was obvious that someone, perhaps being a bit lazy, had taken a picture of Falling Water Creek Falls instead of hiking all the way back to the falls on the larger creek.

I have found an unusually large number of fossils in the rocks below Richland Falls every time I have been to the creek. If you are interested in searching for them, take a little extra time to examine exposed surfaces, particularly around the mouth of Devil's Fork. I once found the imprint of an entire fish skeleton nearby in a two-foot-thick piece of limestone. Flood waters have since moved things around, and I couldn't locate it on my last trip. Maybe you will be lucky enough to find it on your hike.

The valley immediately below Richland Creek Campground is much wider and more open than that above, and the fishing gets better and better as you get closer to the mouth of the creek at the Buffalo River. A rough track of a road follows the stream for over ten miles to the bridge on Highway 74. This makes it easy for an extended hike in that direction for those that are interested. As long as you are in the area, you should stop by a Forestry Service office for maps and directions to the many other scenic spots nearby that await those willing to search them out.

INDEX